# LOVE BEGINS
A Guide to Starting Over
*Cherry Gilchrist and Lara Owen*

# Love Begins at 40

## A Guide to Starting Over

**Cherry Gilchrist** **&** **Lara Owen**

HAY HOUSE
Australia • Canada • Hong Kong • India
South Africa • United Kingdom • United States

First published and distributed in the United Kingdom by:
Hay House UK Ltd, 292B Kensal Rd, London W10 5BE.
Tel.: (44) 20 8962 1230; Fax: (44) 20 8962 1239.
www.hayhouse.co.uk

Published and distributed in the United States of America by:
Hay House, Inc., PO Box 5100, Carlsbad, CA 92018-5100.
Tel.: (1) 760 431 7695 or (800) 654 5126; Fax: (1) 760 431 6948 or (800) 650 5115.
www.hayhouse.com

Published and distributed in Australia by:
Hay House Australia Ltd, 18/36 Ralph St, Alexandria NSW 2015.
Tel.: (61) 2 9669 4299; Fax: (61) 2 9669 4144.
www.hayhouse.com.au

Published and distributed in the Republic of South Africa by:
Hay House SA (Pty), Ltd, PO Box 990, Witkoppen 2068. Tel./Fax: (27) 11 467 8904.
www.hayhouse.co.za

Published and distributed in India by:
Hay House Publishers India, Muskaan Complex, Plot No.3, B-2, Vasant Kunj,
New Delhi – 110 070. Tel.: (91) 11 4176 1620; Fax: (91) 11 4176 1630.
www.hayhouse.co.in

Distributed in Canada by:
Raincoast, 9050 Shaughnessy St, Vancouver, BC V6P 6E5.
Tel.: (1) 604 323 7100; Fax: (1) 604 323 2600

A catalogue record for this book is available from the British Library.
ISBN 978-1-4019-1595-7
Printed and bound in Great Britain by Martins the Printers, Berwick-upon-Tweed.

# Contents

# ACKNOWLEDGEMENTS

We would like to thank everyone who talked to us about their experiences in midlife relationships, and especially the people we interviewed in depth, who were so open and generous with their stories and their time.

We also thank our agent, Doreen Montgomery, for her excellent guidance, and Michelle Pilley and the staff at Hay House for their thoughtful attention and support in bringing this book to fruition.

# Introduction

What do you do when your marriage ends and you find yourself alone in midlife? Or perhaps the right person never came along and you've been single all this time, or busy with your career, or raising children. Perhaps you've been a serial monogamist, always in a relationship of some kind, but never creating a long-term, sustainable bond.

Whatever the causes of you being alone in the middle of your life, what can you do about it now? How do you meet someone when you trudge a daily path between home and work, between home and the supermarket?

It is easy to feel daunted and decide to leave it all up to fate, to think that if a relationship is going to appear, it will knock on your door one night, and all will be well.

Nice try, but this is rarely how relationships begin. When we are young we go to the places other young people go to, and meet our partners there. But in midlife, those places – those clubs and colleges, discos and parties – no longer exist in quite the same way. And even if you have a life that puts you in touch with lots of new people, the current work culture and strictures of professionalism often mean that starting up any romance is out of the question.

So there's no getting around it: to find a relationship in midlife most of us are going to have to do something active about it. But how? And where? What do you do on a first date with someone you know next to nothing about? And what if you do meet someone you like? What then?

We both found ourselves in this position, longing for a relationship but not knowing quite what to do about it. For Cherry, this was following a divorce after a long marriage; for Lara, it came after an early marriage followed by several long-term relationships. Independently, we decided to take steps, and began actively searching.

We met and became friends during this time, and began to share our experiences of Internet searches, newspaper ads and first dates. We had both been frustrated by the lack of helpful literature on this process and on the specific challenges of midlife relationships, so we pooled our resources and experiences in order to understand better what we were going through.

As writers, it was a natural next step to turn what we had learned into a book for others, for the many people who find themselves single in midlife with a lot of love still to give, and who yearn to create a loving, harmonious, sustainable relationship.

Since we began our quests for love we have both found ourselves in new relationships. The value of proactive dating is no longer theoretical to us, but has had a lasting impact on our lives. Each of our journeys has contained its fair share of comedy, embarrassment, anguish and drama, and you'll find some of these stories in the book. We also talked in depth with several of our friends and relations, and other people we met along the way, and we share their stories too.

In each case, at a certain point a decision was made to actively seek a partner. In midlife, without a reproductive drive to impel you into partnership, a relationship has to come from a true desire for genuine intimacy of body and soul, raising the stakes and the requirements for personal development. You need time to get to know a prospective partner, and time to grow into a relationship, because loving in midlife can be scary, and you have a lot to lose. The relative equanimity of being single may be preferable to the risks of falling in love, but this equanimity is achieved at great cost, often the cost of a lonely old age.

And this is why we have written *Love Begins at 40*, to help you find the courage to get out there and date again, and the skill to choose wisely and sustain a partnership through the early hurdles, when it is all too easy to retreat back to the comfort of your own sofa, the bland solace of the television and the unquestioning love of your Labrador.

Instead of retreating, we encourage you to be brave and to honour your desire for love. Yes, it will take some effort, but if you have the willingness to open your heart, refine your strategy, work on your weak spots and persevere in the quest, then success can be yours.

We open in the first chapter with an overview of love and dating in midlife, and touch on the various areas of life that are affected, both the practical everyday issues and the deeper emotions and values involved. The next few chapters are designed to set you up for your search, focusing on how to meet someone and how to manage early dates. But for all the preparation you do ahead of time, many issues won't surface until you are challenged by a new partnership. So in the second half of the book, we look into what those issues are likely to be, and suggest strategies for dealing with them when they come up.

This book is here to help you develop more skill and confidence in all these areas, and is written out of our heartfelt wish for your great happiness and success in your search for love and partnership.

# CHAPTER ONE
## *Love in Midlife*

It's such a huge subject: romantic love. It's both simple and complex at the same time. We know what it feels like, but how do we find it? Sometimes it comes as what seems like a fated bolt from the blue. More often it grows over time, nourished by caring, affection, love-making and thoughtfulness.

After sheer survival, love is the most important element in human life. Love itself comes in many forms: we can gain great sustenance and joy from love of family and children, of pets, of work, of gardens and homes. But for most adults, life is significantly enhanced by romantic love shared with another adult – by love that includes companionship, sex and shared intimacy.

This kind of love can take work, both to find and to keep, and sometimes at midlife it can seem easier to give up on the quest for a happy relationship. But at the same time, we know that our lives are greatly enriched by romance and loving companionship, and so it's worth making the effort to search for this.

## Maturity and the Alchemy of Love

As we grow older, the alchemy of love often shows itself in a softening and opening of the heart. Older people can be capable of a quality of love that can elude the young. It's similar to the love people have for their small children or grandchildren, in that it approaches unconditionality. But here, instead of the parent's remit to shape the child, we find a complete acceptance of the beloved's nature, just as it is. To be loved for who one is, without needing to change anything, is intoxicating and also a huge relief. It makes building a happy life together really possible.

Love is numinous: it changes us. To be with the one we love, we do things we never thought we'd do: we move to new countries, speak new languages, take up new hobbies, make ourselves get along with in-laws and stepchildren, and put up with another person's problems on top of our own. We also find ourselves deeply accepted and supported, adored when we feel unlovable, cared for when we are sick.

Because love has this power to change us and to transform our lives, because it can give us so much, it is imbued with mystical attributes in our collective imagination. This is why we often wait passively for love to happen to us, for a man or woman to appear, with a sense of cosmic inevitability strong enough to propel us into a commitment. In fact, as most mature people will tell you, loving relationships that work for both parties take much more application than just waiting for a thunderbolt to strike. They take hard graft and the willingness to show up on a daily basis. For that you need compatibility as well as the lightning strike of new love and attraction.

And this is where proactive dating can score over random meetings. By making your search conscious and by clearly defining yourself and your aims, you multiply the chances that you will meet someone who is a good fit for you.

## Tolerance and Forgiveness

It's only realistic to understand that it's very rare to be capable of unconditional love all the time. Most of us will experience moments of irritation or frustration with some aspect of our partners and their lives.

Being able to put up with inevitable annoyances, and riding the wave of one's own discomfort, are skills that one can develop in midlife and beyond. It's an element of maturity to become more tolerant of another's foibles, just as we can become more tolerant of our own.

This naturally leads us into the territory of forgiveness. Being able to genuinely forgive another is directly linked into how much we can genuinely forgive ourselves, This means acknowledging cleanly the times when we are insensitive or selfish, and then being able to move on without rancour towards another, or losing confidence in ourselves.

## Growing within a Relationship

We also enter into relationships to grow and to change, to be altered positively by the influence of our partner and the relationship itself. This desire for growth can be part of what attracts us to another person – we sense that they have some aspect of their personality and behaviour that is better developed than our own.

We trade off skills. He teaches her about discipline, she teaches him about spontaneity, for example. One partner is extravagant, the other too thrifty – together they come to a balance in how they relate to money and spending. A lot of this may be unconscious, yet making it conscious can be transformative in terms of relationship harmony.

What we complain about in a partner can be an attribute we could use more of in ourselves. Or it can be something they need to sort out and grow out of, and they have been drawn to us so that we will help them to do that. In good relationships, there is scope for both partners to learn from each other, and to develop in this way.

## Deep Compatibility

When we are young, we think of compatibility in overt terms – fancying each other, doing the same things together, liking the same kinds of fashions, politics, friends, subcultures. As we get older, we often find that deep compatibility is a subtler animal, a matter of soul rather than substance.

If we're lucky, we already have this in our first mate, our original long-term partnership or marriage. But for many of us, the urge for a soul connection (which often arises as midlife approaches) shows up the holes in those early relationships. Divorce ensues, and then we face the search to understand who we are now, what we need now, and what compatibility at 45, 55, 65 actually means.

The term 'soulmate' is often used these days as a marker for a true love. But is deep compatibility the same as the idea of a soulmate? Perhaps, but somewhat surprisingly, given the frequent use of this term in the media and on dating sites, most people we spoke with did not put much stock in the idea of soulmates. Much more common was the notion that a relationship succeeds because people like being with each other, feel deeply comfortable together and want the relationship enough to work on it.

The chief marker for the sustainability of a midlife relationship is real compatibility, whether or not there is a sense of being soulmates. What counts are shared interests, a shared dream for the future and the mutual willingness to compromise in order to create a harmonious and happy life together.

## The Courage to Love Again

Many of us find ourselves in midlife without a partner, for a variety of reasons. We may have never made a long-term bond; we may be bereaved; most likely, though, by this stage in life, we have been divorced. In the UK these days, the average length of marriage of couples divorcing is 11.5 years, which means that many of us will be looking for a new partner by the time we are in our 40s. The average age for divorce is 43 for men and 40 for women. Of all new marriages, 40 per cent involve at least one partner who has been married before.

And it's not surprising, given that one could have a much longer second marriage than first. In most developed countries life expectancy is in the low 80s for women and the mid-70s for men, and many of us will live longer than that. Now 60 is the new 40, and is no longer the gateway to old age. Many people maintain a fit and youthful outlook well past 60, and these days the idea that sex and intimacy lose their place in our lives once we turn the corner into middle age has no currency. So by and large, we no longer think we're 'over the hill' romantically after the age of 40 or 50. We don't buy the idea that it would be undignified or inappropriate to fall in love in midlife. But we are left with two important challenges: how to find a new partner, and how to deal with the complex issues that can arise in a new relationship at this stage in life. These dual problems – the search and the reality – can seem daunting.

Many people say, 'Where on earth will I meet someone?' or 'All the good ones are taken,' or 'What about my children? How can I date in front of them?' Then, if and when you do meet someone you want to make a commitment with, you have to deal with meshing already full schedules, and introducing already formed families to each other. The childless have to deal with stepchildren suddenly appearing in their lives, and with fully grown families with their own culture, habits and preconceptions. It can be hard enough to build a new life with one person, never mind a whole family.

So there are challenges, both in finding someone and in navigating the early stages. But take heart: you can find a partner, if you have the will and the perseverance to keep going with your search. And then, once you've met someone you feel you could have a loving partnership with, the relationship can work – again, if you have the will and perseverance, and if you work together on developing better relationship skills. Relationships are just like anything worth doing: practice, willingness to learn and dedication make all the difference.

And it's worth it, because everyone needs to love and be loved. Here are some stories of people who have been successful at finding and making a new relationship work after 40. You'll continue to meet these people throughout the book, as their tales, our own, and those of other people we met along the way, illustrate the path of midlife love. (With the exception of Lara,

Cherry, and Cherry's partner Robert, names and identifying details throughout the book have been changed to protect the privacy of those involved.)

*Jessica and Evan* live in a leafy suburb of Melbourne, Australia. They met through Match.com, and married two years later. Both in their late 40s, they are self-employed, each with their own small business. Evan's young son, Justin, lives with them for five days every two weeks. Jessica had two prior long-term relationships with partners she found dominating; Evan had been married to Justin's mother, a psychologically disturbed much younger woman. Together, Jessica and Evan have been relieved to find that a deeply intimate and happy relationship is possible after all.

*Adrian and Valerie* live in rural Dorset and urban Birmingham, respectively. Their story is an unusual one, because Adrian was a celibate Buddhist monk for almost two decades before returning to secular life. One of the reasons he left the monastic order was that he felt he wasn't developing or maturing any more, and he wanted to make his own living and have a committed relationship with a woman. Several years later he still hadn't met anyone he felt he could make a life with. A friend recommended dharmamatch.com as a place he might meet a like-minded person, and on his first look at the site he spotted Valerie's profile and immediately had a very good feeling about her. She is an art teacher with two teenage sons, who spend half their time with their father (Valerie's ex-husband), who lives close by. Both in their early 50s, Adrian and Valerie have been dating for a year, just got engaged, and have a long-term plan that will see them living together once Valerie's younger son finishes school.

*Peter and Anna* live in Paris, and met through work. He was 48 and she was 19. Peter had been divorced ten years earlier after a problematic and childless first marriage. He had never really recovered emotionally, subsequently dating a series of women but never able to commit. He wasn't happy with the bachelor lifestyle, and knew he really wanted a partner. He was very attracted to Anna but extremely wary of the age difference. Unusually mature for her age, she was convinced from the beginning that he was her man. They waited a year before getting involved, until they were both sure the feelings they had for each other were real. Quite quickly, Anna became pregnant and so they married, and now are the happy parents of a little boy. Despite Peter's initial misgivings, they are very content together and he is grateful for Anna's calm persistence in the face of his doubts.

*Hannah and Hugh* live together in Reading, where Hannah runs a family business and Hugh teaches at a local college. They plan to marry soon. Now in their early 50s, both had been previously married with children. After their respective divorces, they had each searched assiduously through Internet sites and had gone on a lot of dates before meeting each other through Guardian Soulmates. They found that being authentic was a large part of their individual journeys to finding a partner. Spirituality and personal development are very important to them, and to support their relationship and grow as individuals, they have gone on many couples' workshops and trained in Tantric sexuality.

*Stephanie and Martin* met on a walking holiday. At the time, Stephanie was living in the north of England and had been on her own for about ten years, bringing up her three children while holding down a demanding job as a head teacher. Martin was a lecturer in the Midlands whose wife had died of cancer a few years before. Stephanie had been out with a few men since her divorce, including some she met through personal ads and a dating agency, but thought she had left it too late now she was in her mid-50s. But when Martin, a few years older, joined the same holiday that she had booked to Italy, romance blossomed on the slopes of Mount Vesuvius, and they married 15 months later. Despite some fundamental differences – Stephanie follows a Buddhist meditation practice, while Martin is an atheist – they have a harmonious and happy relationship.

*Kate and Douglas*, both in their mid-60s, met through an introduction agency and married four years later after living together for a couple of years. Kate had previously been married for 27 years, and has two grown-up sons. She had a relationship with a younger man for a while after her divorce, which gave her confidence but ultimately couldn't go any further. Douglas had been married twice before, the first time briefly and straight out of university, the second a much longer marriage in which he and his wife brought up two daughters. Although he wanted a new partnership, he would have been extremely reluctant to actively search for one had it not been for the recommendation of a colleague, who had found his own partner through the same agency. Kate and Douglas both feel that they were lucky to meet at all, since without the agency their paths would never have crossed.

*Anthony and Claudia* were in their late and early 60s respectively when they met through an introduction agency based in the West Country. Anthony had been widowed five years earlier, after a long and happy marriage. Claudia had been married twice before, and has two grown-up daughters from her first marriage, and a teenage granddaughter. She was no stranger to personal ads and agencies, having married her second husband through meeting him this way. However, that marriage was not a success, which made her wary of future involvements. Anthony signed up to the agency, determined to receive good service from them and find a partner; Claudia decided to give it one last shot, but had no high expectations. At their first meeting, Anthony was convinced 'She was the one.' It took Claudia a few months to be sure, but they have been happily together ever since, and married three years after they first met.

## The Proactive Approach

As you'll see from these stories, some of these couples met through the proactive approach (dating sites, agencies, ads) and some met through everyday life. But all of them were focused on wanting to meet someone.

The old adage states: 'God will provide, but you must lay your own knife and fork.' On the other hand, people may say to you,

'It will happen when you're not looking for it.' This may or may not be true, but only after you've 'laid your knife and fork'. Taking an active approach prepares the ground. It opens the heart and is likely to lead you, sooner or later, to your loved one. It will almost certainly bring you new, rich and interesting experiences.

Cherry had lived on her own for four years after her marriage ended before she decided that she would like to find a new partner.

*During that period, my thoughts about another relationship had gone from 'Not interested' to 'If it happens, well and good.' Then I literally woke up one morning and realized, 'I have to make an effort. It's not going to happen unless I do.' It dawned on me that there was no point in just waiting around. I wasn't meeting anyone new through work or other interests and, in fact, I couldn't remember the last time I had met an available man of a suitable age. I was 54 years old, and it was time to get moving. I had to be proactive.*

And so Cherry dated using the Internet and ads for a few years, at one point having a serious relationship for 18 months – but one that was always problematic and caused her some heartache.

*After that there were a few more meetings, including some promising encounters, but nothing quite gelled. I had just decided to join a reputable introduction agency when I met Robert.*

*As it happened, we came across each other on a cruise, where we were both working as guest lecturers. Within a few months we were living together, and now, a year later, are planning to marry. Did this happen by chance? I think not. I believe that my period of proactive dating was the fuel that got me to the right time and place where we could find each other. It prepared me, and taught me to recognize true love when it came along.*

Proactive dating is all part of creating your own luck, helping your life along. Sometimes people comment that it feels soulless and manufactured; too much like relationship 'shopping'. But in fact, being proactive about meeting a partner can be a vehicle for our emotional and spiritual values. Several of our interviewees used their ideals and life-skills consciously when they dated proactively. Jessica, a psychotherapist, devised a kind and elegant way to end blind dates (whether or not she was attracted to the person), saying that she would take a little time to think and allow her impressions to sink in, and would contact them soon. Valerie said a prayer when she first went on the Internet site, to guide her search. And Adrian, our ex-Buddhist monk, used all of his sensitivity when he crafted his first email to Valerie: 'I wanted to write a letter that had to be answered, that wouldn't put her off nor fail to engage her romantic attention.' It worked, even though Valerie was just about to give up the whole business of Internet dating as a dead loss. (Interestingly, several of our interviewees met the love of their life just as they were about to give up.)

So there are ways of being creative and mindful when using proactive dating: it can make the process feel more like you, rather than being depersonalized and as if you are on a conveyor belt. These days, dating sites and agencies are developing all the time, new ways of dating like dining clubs and speed dating are being devised, and the old prejudices against meeting this way are going for good.

## Advantages of Proactive Dating

- You meet a wider range of people than you'd find in your immediate circle.

- The people you meet also have an active interest in establishing a relationship.

- It's permitted to ask leading questions about what they're looking for.

- You can approach it in a structured way.

- You can choose your own timing as to when to do it.

- You can make new friends along the way.

- It may open your eyes to the possibility of a different type of partner or relationship than you had previously considered.

- It can get you going on the dating scene again and boost your confidence.

## Disadvantages of Proactive Dating

- There is no context to place the person in, so you can't easily check them out gradually in their social or work setting before going on a date.

- You may need to verify their details – e.g. age, occupation and, in extreme cases, even their genuine identity.

- The pressure of the date can make both parties nervous, which can lessen attractiveness.

- The stated aim of seeking a relationship can become

something of a heavy agenda which one or other person finds difficult to handle.

- It costs money.

## The Three Core Values

There are three core values in the quest for love: authenticity, practicality and wisdom.

### Authenticity

In midlife you know who you are, and if you fully own that, you can present yourself with greater personal power and integrity than when you were young and relatively unformed.

### Practicality

The quest for love at midlife demands some practical effort; it demands a commitment to the search, and a deliberate focus on finding a partner.

### Wisdom

At midlife you bring decades of experience to the table, and while these past experiences can include emotional issues that still need to be worked on, you also have more knowledge about how relationships work and about what you need in a partner.

## The Relationship Quest

We can think of the relationship quest as a tree. It has roots that go deep into the soil: these are the roots of wisdom, created from all the experiences you have had in life up to now, and from your connection to the source within yourself, and to the greater source of life energy that infuses all of us.

Then there is the stem, the trunk, the sturdy spine of the relationship. This manifests through the practical realm, through everything you do to make a relationship work in the day-to-day, and in terms of your quest, through all that you do to make it successful, from advertising your desire for a partner to updating your wardrobe.

The leaves and branches, the flowering crown of the tree, are shown outwardly in how you greet the world, and it is here that authenticity and honesty become paramount. If you meet the world, and the potential partners out there, with the genuine self-confidence that arises naturally out of authenticity, then you will become magnetic and draw someone suitable towards you. Such a person, attracted honestly and clearly, will match your being and be a fitting partner for you.

So, if you are not afraid to show yourself for who you are, while at the same time being supported by your practical commitment and rooted in your life experience, then your chances of finding a compatible partner whom you can respect as much as you clearly respect yourself, become very strong indeed.

## Developing Relationship Skills for Midlife

Throughout this book you'll find an emphasis on skilful means – on ways of entering into relationships in midlife with intelligence and awareness. It's not enough simply to have an open heart, even if you've managed to keep your heart open despite past disappointment. An open heart can just mean you constantly fall in love with people who can't return your love for one reason or another.

So while it is tremendously important to keep your heart open and, in a sense, innocent, you also need to focus on being skilful in navigating the various pitfalls of midlife love. This combination of heart and skill can turn around your relationship fate and experience.

These skills relate to the three core values just mentioned; the values are not just the starting point for your search, but are key themes that weave their way through the book. Take note of them, as they can help you enormously along the way.

## Authenticity Skills

These include self-knowledge, self-acceptance, self-confidence and clear communication. It means knowing who you are and are not, what you need, what you want, and what does and doesn't work for you, without being rigid or self-limiting. These skills of personal awareness go a long way to your being able to find a partner who suits you.

*Lara: When I first tried Internet dating I thought I should present myself as someone generally appealing, so I downplayed my deep interest in spirituality and personal development in my description of myself. So yes, I got tons of responses, but all from men who weren't a good fit. When I adjusted my profile to reflect my authentic nature, I got fewer replies, but I was amazed to find how many men turned up with the same interests as mine.*

Hannah, one of our interviewees, runs a large family business and found she never met anyone like-minded in her work environment. She is deeply interested in astrology and psychology. She found that many of the men she met through Internet dating sites would roll their eyes when she mentioned astrology. Rather than hiding this interest, she went the other way and decided to make that a priority, making it one of her compatibility keywords. Shortly after this she met Hugh, who didn't know much about astrology but who was interested in learning more, and wanted to find a woman who was spiritually inclined and open-minded to the whole arena of self-development:

*We've been together for nearly two years now. He moved in with me after a year, and we're doing really well. It's so much more harmonious, and so much more interesting, than my previous relationships, and I think that's because I was so uncompromising about how I presented myself. If I had played down my interests I wouldn't have been attractive to Hugh, because he wanted a partner who would be into exploring this stuff with him.*

## Practical Skills

These include how to meet people looking for love, how to manage dates, and how to deal with the practical elements of the early stages of a midlife relationship. At midlife, meeting someone can be a practical challenge, given the demands of children and work. And once you have met someone, the practical issues of managing different priorities can be daunting and need clear thinking to figure out.

Many of our interviewees noted that they found few opportunities for meeting suitable partners.

Jessica worked as a psychotherapist, so most of the new people she met were clients, and she couldn't date them. On her days off she tended to spend time relaxing with her parents, sisters or long-standing women friends, most of whom complained of the same problem. 'You can't just walk up to a nice-looking guy in the street and ask him out.'

Hannah's job in her family business meant she met a lot of men, but they were either married or just not the kind of men she felt she would be compatible with.

If you were thinking of buying a car, and there weren't any obviously available, you wouldn't just sit at home and wait for one to turn up in the driveway. No, you'd get onto the Internet and do a search for the car you wanted, or look in the local paper. What you would not do is sit at home grumbling about the lack of cars in the world.

## Wisdom Skills

These include dealing constructively with conflict, not having unreasonable expectations, having high enough expectations, knowing your bottom line, and being aware of your standards. Wisdom lets us know what is really important for our health and happiness, and what we can let go of. As we mature into tolerant and respectful human beings, we learn not to confuse our own needs with those we've been conditioned into. The lessons of the years can also help in discriminating between potential partners, and further down the road in moving through the inevitable glitch moments when a relationship momentarily falters in front of an obstacle. Wisdom helps us know when and how we can adjust to another's expectations, and how to deliver what is needed without compromising our own values and needs.

In the first year of her relationship with Evan, Jessica seriously questioned whether or not she should stay in the relationship. Yes, she loved him, but there seemed to be so many problems. She despaired over the way Evan's unruly seven-year-old, Justin, was being brought up, indulged by both parents and used by his mother as a pawn in her continuing demands for more money (money that Evan didn't have, already stretched to the max by the maintenance he was paying).

Jessica decided to go back into therapy. 'It was so confronting, the whole situation. I knew I couldn't handle it on my own, and Evan was so embroiled in the difficulties that he couldn't see the wood for the trees half the time.'

Therapy helped Jessica find more confidence in her own wisdom about what everyone needed. She talked to Evan about the need to establish clearer boundaries with Justin, to gently bring some discipline into his life. They rearranged the child-sharing arrangement so that it was less disruptive to Justin, giving him longer stretches with each parent.

Jessica had the wisdom to know that essentially her relationship with Evan was worth working at, but that at a crucial stage she couldn't handle her side of things without help. Her therapist helped Jessica access her own wisdom about what needed to be done to make the situation work better for everyone.

## Common Issues in Midlife Relationships

### *Timing*

When you meet someone, the way you manage the early stages with them can play a big part in the success of the relationship. Rushing at the beginning can put a potential partner off, especially if they have been hurt or let down in the past. They may not trust declarations of love that appear as if out of nowhere. If one or both of you aren't ready, and yet you sense the relationship really has possibilities for long-term happiness, you may have to be patient.

It can be tempting to leap into a new relationship fast. Sometimes this works out very well, as in the case of Cherry and Robert, who were both genuinely ready and very compatible. Their lives could mesh together easily because their children were grown up and they work for themselves as a writer and an artist respectively.

But there are instances when hot-housing a new relationship, instead of allowing it to develop more slowly, can mean you end up tied in with someone who has problems you hadn't been aware of, or with whom you discover you have serious incompatibilities.

If you've been lonely for a long time it can be tempting to spend all your time together right away. This can result in a kind of claustrophobia that may feel smothering for one partner, and cause the destruction of what could have been a good relationship.

Moving in together too soon can mean you find yourself tied to someone who is a liability, or with whom you just don't get along well enough to warrant that depth of commitment.

Being older can make us feel impatient, and impose a sense that we need to get together in a rush. Every relationship has its own pattern, and sometimes we need to dig deep and access patience and wisdom to allow deepening intimacy to proceed at a comfortable pace.

## Prior Commitments

As we saw above in the example from Jessica's life, children can be a major factor to deal with in forming a new relationship in midlife. Other commitments that often loom large during this life phase are ageing parents, work, studies, friends, houses, gardens and pets. It's a good idea to be realistic about which of these are non-negotiable for you, while not letting them stop you from moving forward with your romantic life.

Sometimes people don't even begin to date because they can't see how they will deal with their children and a new partner, or find the time for a relationship in a busy working life. But with imagination, optimism and foresight, we can manage the complexities that arise, and often things can then improve for everyone. Jessica's insights into Justin's needs have helped him become a more settled little boy.

In many cases, we need to be prepared to make some changes to accommodate a new relationship. Again, patience is a key factor here. Expecting everything to be perfect right from the word go is even more unlikely in midlife than it was when you were young and had far fewer prior commitments.

## Managing Assets

We enter into relationships in midlife already owning houses, cars, stock portfolios, and also often carrying debt and having dependants. So how much we pool our resources is an issue that needs to be constructively and consciously examined. While existing commitments may have to be honoured, they may also need to be changed in the light of a new relationship. Sometimes it is easiest to keep things simple and maintain separate bank accounts and even homes, options that we'll explore further on in this book. But if we can't afford to do this, or don't wish to, then merging the material aspects of our lives becomes a task that demands sensitivity and intelligence.

## Future Dreams

By midlife we are aware of what we have achieved, and of what we still long to accomplish. How much have we lived up to our potential? New relationships can help or hinder our development and also our ability to live in the ways that make us happiest. Talking together about how you see the future can be important both for bonding and also for clarifying if you really fit together as a couple. Can you move forward into the future together? Are your dreams compatible?

## Maintaining Your Balance

Getting into a new relationship in midlife might be exciting, but it can also feel quite daunting and destabilizing. It's almost bound to bring changes and challenges to the existing structures of your life, whether these are to do with your family, your finances or your friendships.

If you allow for this and realize that the results are not necessarily going to be instantaneous and simple, you'll navigate the changes much more easily.

As several of our interviewees found, at crucial times therapy and counselling helped them get through potential trouble spots and find new and creative ways of dealing with difficulties.

Others used couple-orientated groups and workshops to deepen their connection and help them work through issues. The support of religious organizations and spiritual practice can help to foster the compassion and understanding that are often needed. And there is nothing like the warm-hearted common sense of trusted friends to see us through tricky times. A new relationship in midlife, however wonderful, still requires us to keep up the support systems that we're used to, as well as drafting in extra help if necessary.

In this chapter we've seen how midlife relationships often bring up more complex issues than relationships formed when we are younger. It can seem more difficult to meet someone and, once we've met them, our more complex life structures have to be dealt with and often incorporated into the new relationship.

But this shouldn't stop us from moving forward optimistically and finding new love. If we can engage with these challenges intelligently and proactively, we stand a great chance of finding lasting love and creating a sustainable relationship that really suits us.

In the next chapter we're going to look at how to prepare for finding your new relationship. We've identified seven key questions for clarifying your relationship needs. Focusing on these seven keys will help you launch into your search.

CHAPTER TWO

# *The Seven Keys:*
# *Your Aims for a New*
# *Relationship*

*When you're younger, you fall in love and you think about family,*
*children, settling down and repeating what your parents did – or not.*
*When you're older you're looking for different things. You're actually*
*looking for a real partner.*

This is how Dawn, an art therapist in her mid-40s, views her
search for love in her current situation. In midlife there is often a
welcome freedom from the expectations that are present earlier
in life. There is a chance to redefine what you would like from
a relationship. We might value our past relationships, but when
we find ourselves single again in midlife we may also be keen to
move forward, to learn from our past mistakes and evolve in our
capacity to give and receive love.

So are you ready to take the plunge? Perhaps you've decided
that you'd like a new relationship and it's time to get started. All
those other people seem to be swimming up and down in the pool
and enjoying themselves. The water looks inviting, and you've been
hanging around on the edge for too long. Why not just jump in?

You can indeed, but it's a good idea to begin by focusing on your aims. While enthusiasm is a great motivator, your search is likely to go better if you prepare yourself first. Jumping straight in may be energizing, and people are likely to respond well if you are lively and enthusiastic about meeting them, but raw enthusiasm can burn out all too quickly unless you are prepared and practical. You leap into the water and it's colder than you thought; someone knocks into you just as you're starting to swim, and you're not sure you've got the stamina to keep going. Soon you're scrambling out of the pool and reaching for your towel.

When you start on this search, the chances are that you'll need to understand something about your needs and your capacity in the area of relationships. This helps you go forward with confidence, and keep faith with the quest even if the going gets tough. So it's a good idea to begin by figuring out your aims and preparing your search. Taking an objective view in this way should actually help to safeguard your capacity for joy and spontaneity, qualities which will help you along the way.

## THE SEVEN KEY QUESTIONS

Here are seven points to consider in defining your aims. We suggest that you take time to go through each one, perhaps reviewing one a day for a week, and jotting down any thoughts that come to you. They are all significant, but while some may need exploring at length, others may be simpler for you to answer. With some questions you may not come to a fixed conclusion, or will need to allow time for your thoughts to evolve. But contemplating them now will lay a good foundation for your search. You will also be setting up prompts for yourself, bells that may ring in warning if you're veering away from these aims too much, or perhaps chiming harmoniously if a new friendship is more in accord with your fundamental aims.

With all these questions and answers, keep some degree of flexibility in your expectations. This means that you are allowing space for another person to come into your life, for pleasant surprises and for the magic that arises between you. For now, focusing on these aims relates primarily to you, and is about clarifying your own preferences and intentions. Later on in the book we'll be considering what happens when we encounter other people's agendas, and how to negotiate the interaction. But looking first at your own goals will be very helpful when you begin your journey, and will give you a sense of security to support you on the way.

These are questions for you, and you only, to decide. Everyone else may have views on exactly what you should do – friends, relatives and even your children are probably only too ready to give you good advice – but in this case, too many cooks spoil the broth, and the answer lies in your own heart. We'll be talking later about how to ask the people in your life for help and feedback, but the basis of your search is something for you alone to contemplate.

## 1. What Kind of Relationship Do You Want?

This is a big topic, and takes up more space than some of the other subjects on the list. Let's start with the question of whether you would like to have a long-term relationship or not, and the options which go along with that.

## Marriage or Partnership? NO

Would you like to get married? Some people are already crystal-clear in their intention. 'I want a wife,' declared one man to Cherry on a first date. Others are more wary; Claudia had no intention of getting married again before she met Anthony. She valued her independence, hard-won after an unhappy second marriage. 'That was the biggest learning curve for me – finding that you can be more alone in a marriage than just being on your own. Unfortunately, it took seven years out of my life to understand that.' But after she began seeing Anthony, she realized that here was a man she could trust absolutely, and although she kept the pace steady, she finally accepted his proposal of marriage. Speaking shortly before they tied the knot, she said, 'It just feels right. It's that final step.' She feels that the commitment of a long-term relationship is not as great as that of marriage. 'If we hit dodgy patches, if we weren't finally committed with that piece of paper, it could be very easy to walk away and perhaps not work at what's gone off at a tangent.'

Marriage can be a 'yes', a 'no' or a 'maybe' at this point. You may feel it's too early even to be considering this, but if you do go down the route of proactive dating, it may come up sooner than you think. In this context, people tend to discuss their aims and objectives more frankly than they would in the usual social arena. You may also be asked the question during an interview if you sign up to an introduction agency.

You may prefer to focus your search on looking for a long-term partner rather than a spouse. The social pressures to marry for the sake of children, or to please one's parents, are rarely as strong at this stage in life. Commitment to a partnership can be a serious and whole-hearted business, but may also leave each person room to appreciate some degree of autonomy, perhaps over financial affairs or living arrangements. Further down the line, if you are considering whether to get married or simply remain partners, it would be wise to take legal advice on questions of property, finances or inheritance, and we'll be touching on this in the final chapter of the book.

## Two Roofs or One?

Not all long-term relationships begun in mid- or later life involve living together. Some monogamous, permanent partnerships can flourish well in what is commonly known as LAT (Living Apart Together). A survey run in 2006 by *Saga* magazine from their over-50s readership produced a flood of responses from LATs eager to tell their success stories. Some couples lived at a distance from one another and enjoyed visiting each other's houses, creating quite a holiday atmosphere. Others preferred to be able to make their own mess in their own kitchen, keep their finances separate and even heat their houses to the temperature they personally liked.

Habits, comfort and domestic stability do count for something in the second half of life, especially when great efforts may have been made to re-establish one's life after a painful divorce or bereavement. Before she met Douglas, Kate thought that she might like a 'two roofs' relationship, and Anthony and Claudia, who are now married, still keep two houses. Other examples from people we know include a jazz player who is happy to see his lady only once every two weeks, and a teacher who is only now taking steps to move from her busy life in Devon to live part-time in London with her partner of 12 years' standing.

Midlife can be a chance to create anew, but not necessarily by throwing out the whole way of life that you have built up. A wise appraisal of your own needs and habits will help to keep your aims authentic and realistic, and in time lead to a way of life that will suit you and your partner.

## Romance, Sex and Friendly Company

If you are not sure that you want a long-term relationship just yet, or if you are looking for something less committed, then this can also form the basis of your intention.

'It's the romance I want now. I don't really want the day-to-day hassle,' Dawn remarked. Although she would like a new partner, and has met men via the Internet, she admits that she is not quite ready to take the step into full partnership. This is primarily because she is still bringing up and supporting two teenage children. But it took a couple of serious involvements with men who wanted to make a permanent commitment to her – one even wanted her to have his baby – before she acknowledged this to herself. Finding out what we do or don't want through first-hand experience is inevitably a part of the process, but it can also be painful. You can make it somewhat easier for yourself by thinking these questions through first, and being as honest with yourself as possible.

So if you would like a series of romantic dates, perhaps a fling or two, or just a 'from time to time' relationship, be ready to acknowledge that. It is not a crime, and rediscovering both romance and sexuality are often a part of the journey towards a long-term relationship and finding a permanent partner.

It's also possible to have a very pleasant companionship with a member of the opposite sex without physical intimacy. Some newspapers run a special section for finding a friend on this basis. Dawn didn't rule this out for herself: 'I met a nice man from Wales, but there was no spark on my side.' She thought they might have been good company for one another, but he wasn't prepared to do that. 'He said at first he would be happy to be friends, but on second meeting it was clear that he wasn't, which disappointed me.'

And sometimes a relaxed friendship can lead to more. Margaret, a woman writer who had been widowed relatively young, in her 50s, decided to join a dating agency back in the 1980s. She was adamant that she was only looking for a male friend to go on holiday with. The travelling partner that she found this way later persuaded her to marry him, and they have now lived happily together for some 18 years.

If you are not really up for a serious involvement, then feel free to admit this – you are likely to have fewer awkward complications, and if you can keep the door open to possible developments, you may be pleasantly surprised one day.

## 2. How Do You See Your Own Future?

Where do you feel that your life is going? You probably have ideas about where your work or retirement activities are leading, where you wish to live in the future, and what you hope to achieve during the rest of your life. (We'll look at family situations in the next section.) Although the plans that you have now may well be modified by any new relationship, it's still a good idea to think them through and decide which aspects you would or would not in principle be happy to change.

## Work

If you are working, would you be prepared to change or give up your job if needs be? There are many circumstances within a new partnership that might cause this question to arise, such as the need for one of you to relocate, or your partner's health, age and so on.

If it's a 'no,' then this means that, for whatever reason, your work takes prime position in your life. So if you meet someone through proactive dating, it is only fair to let him or her know early on that you are going to follow your career through. It is only fair on yourself too, since it would be tragic to find new love only to have to renounce it later on because of the incompatibility of your circumstances.

If your answer is a 'yes' or a 'maybe', then you have maximum flexibility when it comes to establishing a new relationship. You are aware that situations can change, and that a relationship may alter your priorities.

Kate had planned to go on with her satisfying career until retirement, but not long after she and Douglas met and made their commitment to each other he had a spell of illness which meant that he had to give up work, and they could no longer take it in turns to commute the 50 miles or so to each other's houses or develop a long-term plan to live together over a period of time. It was an all-or-nothing situation, and Kate decided that her feelings for Douglas were strong enough to accelerate the process; she gave up her job and moved into his home as, for practical reasons, hers wasn't suitable for Douglas while he was unwell. In the end it all worked out very well. They bought a joint house together in a new location a little later on, and are now happy in the category of 'busy retired' together. But if Kate had not been willing or able to give up her job, it would have been the end of the line for them as a couple.

Even if no difficult events come your way to change your plans, a new partnership may change your outlook anyway. Stephanie was working as a head teacher in a special needs school when she met Martin; he was a full-time lecturer, and for a while they whizzed backwards and forwards between their respective cities at weekends. Once again though, all worked out well. Martin took partial retirement, moved to be with Stephanie and, after a year of living together, Stephanie realized that they weren't spending enough time together while she was still in full-time employment. After a great summer holiday she suddenly thought, 'I don't really want to go back to work. I'll make this my last year at school.'

So a 'maybe' is not an evasion; it can be a mature outlook, knowing that where you are now, and how you feel, can be changed somewhere down the line. None of us can predict all the circumstances that will arise, or how our feelings may develop within a new and loving relationship. Be prepared to let the alchemy of love do its work.

## Where You Live

On the question of relocation, would you be prepared to move to be with your partner? This is not to say that you have to be the one in the relationship to uproot, but would you actually consider doing so?

*Cherry: I always felt that there were limits on where I was willing to live. I used to say to my friends that no new love would be powerful enough to tempt me to live in an industrial city hundreds of miles away! When I met Robert, however, he was living in Belfast. This wasn't a place I was drawn to, but I realized that because of the strength of our relationship, I'd be willing to move there, for a few years at least.*

As things worked out, in the end Robert chose to join Cherry in Bath where she was living at the time.

However, it may be impossible or extremely difficult for you to move if you have children or other commitments. If you can't move, or won't consider it, then again this is something to make clear at an early point in your new relationship. Remember, too, that this will restrict your choice of relationship; if you can't find the love of your life on your doorstep, then you might need to be open to a long-distance relationship, or else look for a partner who is willing to move to be with you.

## Spiritual Values

What are your spiritual values? Do you practise a religious faith which makes particular demands on your calendar or way of life? If so, then this is likely to be a non-negotiable aspect of your life, and you will need to be with someone who fully understands this if he or she is not of your own religion.

If you follow a spiritual path which is essential to your life, but which is outside the main religious structures, this is also relevant to your aims in finding a new relationship. If you need to set time aside regularly, inside or outside the home, for meditation, group work or retreats, for instance, then this needs to be acknowledged by your partner. He or she may not follow the same practices as you, but does at least need to respect them, and accept the time and space that they occupy.

'Martin is an atheist and has always been so,' says Stephanie, who practises and teaches Buddhist meditation. 'He is rather fazed by the Buddhism, but it doesn't create issues between us; it was part of the package. And he has now been on a weekend on "Meditation for the Curious"!'

Of course, the same question applies in reverse: what type of belief, or lack of it, would you accept in a partner?

## 3. What About Your Role in the Family?
*Children*

If you have dependent children, you will already be well aware of this as an issue in the search for love. Sometimes, however, people launch into dating hoping optimistically that all these issues will resolve themselves by the power of love itself.

Dawn had a steady relationship with a man she met through the Internet, and spent a year seeing him. 'It was an escape. I went away every other weekend and my children stayed with their father. But it started to jar after a while. The two worlds didn't really meet.' She introduced the new man to her children as a friend, but ultimately she wasn't comfortable with the situation, and ended it. Since then, she has felt the need to keep relationships very light-hearted, unless she meets a man with whom she intends to share her future. She hopes that this will happen one day.

At this point in preparing for proactive dating, you don't have to work out every possible strategy for dealing with relationships and children, but it's worth asking yourself whether you can take on a relationship in these circumstances and, if so, how you would need to shape it. (We'll go more deeply into the theme of existing family commitments later on in the book.)

## Elderly Parents and Caring for Others

If you have parents, relatives, grandchildren or friends whom you regularly look after in some way, then this will affect the resources that you have available for a relationship. What amount of time could you actually spare for a relationship? Would your caring role influence how much time you could spend on holiday with a partner, for instance? Will you be able to give your lover priority in your life?

Ed, a successful lawyer who was meeting women through personal ads, announced on his dates that he had two grown-up children living with him at home, a wife with a violent personality disorder just down the road (who had once fractured his skull with an iron cooking pan), and a mother with Alzheimer's. He also made it clear that he considered it his duty in life to look after them all. This was an honest and honourable declaration, but it did not put him in a very good position in respect of a new relationship. Few women would be prepared to commit to a man in these circumstances. Unfortunately, he did not seem to recognize this and, had he thought it through more carefully, he might have taken steps to make genuine space in his life for a new partner, for instance by getting a divorce and moving to a place of his own in a new neighbourhood.

## The Other Person's Dependents

In midlife, the people we meet often have complicated lives, and it's useful to recognize the limits of what we are prepared to take on. If you have finished bringing up your own children and never want to go through it again, then a prospective partner who has full-time dependant children is probably not a good fit for you. However, do also consider whether part-time contact with your partner's children might in fact be rewarding. Rebecca, a woman in her 40s who has never wanted children of her own, is happy to help with her partner's ten-year-old son at weekends, and this has led to a lot of enjoyable days out together.

If the children aren't young, consider if you would cope well with older offspring hanging around the home, commandeering the sound system and expecting regular feeding sessions. Of course, it might be a lot nicer than this! But there again, it might not. You can't cover every eventuality in advance, but you can probably work out where you would draw the line, and this may in turn rule out various possible relationships.

## 4. How Much Independence Do You Want?

By the second half of life, many men and women living on their own have created a stable base for themselves, and are used to making decisions without having to refer to their 'other half'.

When Kate was looking for a new partner after her divorce, she questioned whether she wanted to give up the life she had created for herself. 'Being on my own was hard initially, but then I started to enjoy my own company, and learn how to manage my own time.' She wanted to be part of a loving couple again, but for the relationship to be based on interdependence, rather than dependence. 'Being on your own also teaches you to cope, to manage DIY jobs and other aspects of your life that someone else has handled before.'

This is a chance to appraise your own situation candidly. Do you in fact prefer being on your own? For some people, a partnership can actually create an unwelcome confinement; if you feel this way, then maybe it is not for you, or perhaps you would find it easier to have a more casual relationship.

Most of us need some degree of independence and time to ourselves in a relationship, and this is also worth thinking about at the outset. Anthony and Claudia have bought a house together, but are lucky enough to be able to keep Anthony's own property as well, a beautiful and spacious house by the sea. They spend most of their time together, but have certain periods apart when Anthony, a former ship's captain, actively enjoys his solitude. 'It's part of being a mariner. Seafarers are on their own a lot in the job; they tend to be rather lone souls, and I'm happy with that. I can sit in the house for several days on my own and not worry.'

## 5. What Is Your Key Intention?

So far, the questions we've explored here have been logical ones. They may be centred around burning issues and throw up powerful emotions, but they help us to think about the situation in a practical and rational way. Now it's time to answer from the heart: What is your intention? What are you really looking for?

Answering from the heart means allowing your deepest desires to speak. This allows you to connect with your essential being and with what is true and authentic for you. It takes the quest out of the realm of mere chance and helps you to create your own luck, allowing love to manifest in your life.

The simpler the intention, the better. The more it is cluttered with 'ifs' and 'buts', the more sub-clauses it contains, then the more complexity you are introducing and the more likely you are to be confused by the relative merits of the people you meet. The essence of a good relationship is actually very simple.

You might formulate something like these examples:

- *I wish to find a loving, committed relationship.*
- *I would like to find a new partnership with room for personal independence.*
- *I wish to meet someone to enjoy the rest of my life with.*
- *I want a lover who shares my spiritual values.*

Going simple can be hard! If a number of intentions or desires spring to mind, write them all down to start with. See if they are in fact pointing towards one direction, towards one clear intention. Or hold them gently in your mind and come back to the question later. Please note that it can be awfully scary making the statement that you are looking for love. (After all, then it might actually happen.)

## Secret Wishes

You may find that other wishes pop up in your mind, ones which might seem based more on practical issues and less on the ideal of love, such as a desire for financial support or for a new father for your children. These are not unworthy, and may arise out of genuine practical need. Give yourself time to reflect upon them, and if one of them is your true priority, then acknowledge it as such.

Sometimes our desires come from emotional needs that may be hard for anyone to meet. If you want a partner who worships you, or someone who displays affection constantly, what you are asking for may be difficult to find. Again, such desires are not wrong, but would you actually be satisfied if you achieved them? Remember, too, that a good relationship is based on mutuality, and what you ask of your partner you should in some way be able to offer in return. Can you give in return the support that you crave, for instance? Will you be able to return such unquestioning adoration in all moods and weathers?

Acknowledge your wishes and desires, but expect that some of them will recede to lesser importance. Even if they seem intense and tenacious, they may just be indicators of what you're looking for, pointing to something deeper and more in accord with the truth of your quest. Keep on mulling until you are really sure that you have formulated the intention that is right for you. You will usually know, because it often brings a sense of happiness and peace with it. 'Aha, so that's what I really want!'

### Fixing Your Aim

When you have found the best formulation of your intention, then fix it by writing it down. If you like, you can choose a small  stone to represent it; hold it while you speak the intention out loud. The stone then symbolizes your aim, and you can keep it in your pocket or bag, have it by your bed or wherever you please. It is literally a 'touchstone'. Each time you hold it or look at it, you can think about what it represents. The path to your relationship may be a curving one, and there can be surprises and disappointments along the way. We can sometimes feel further away from the goal than ever, but this is often part of the journey, as the road twists and turns. Staying in touch with your key aim will help you to know whether you have gone off-course or if you just need to be patient and persistent for a while longer. It's possible that the intention may need to be re-stated in a different form at some stage, but stick with the original unless you are absolutely sure that it needs updating. Have trust in the quest.

## 6. What Qualities Would You Like in a Partner?

Now that you have done the core work of clarifying your situation and defining your aim, you can relax and think about the type of person you hope to meet. Be playful! It's part of the fun of proactive dating. You can make the safe choices of the 'kind, caring, intelligent' type, but you can also be imaginative, experimental and even outrageous if you like. This is the time to stretch your imagination.

### New Hopes, Old Patterns

There is a good reason for allowing your fancy to fly free as you consider who and what a new lover might be. From the age of 40 onwards, most people have had a live-in or long-term relationship, and our patterns of expectation, of what we do and don't like, have become somewhat fixed. Perhaps some of those will remain – maybe your love of a practical man or a lively, witty woman is part of who you are. But you might, next time round, be prepared to consider a mystical man or a quiet, thoughtful woman, who doesn't fit your normal model. Open up your horizons; this will prepare you to meet a range of different people in early dates, even if you do become more selective later on.

### The Non-negotiable Factor

Despite being as open-minded as you can, you will probably have one or two non-negotiable factors in terms of what you are looking for in a partner. 'He must be taller than me!' 'I want a woman who shares my love of sailing,' 'I will only go out with a man who has been to university.' Strangely enough, it is these fixed ideas that usually fly out of the window when you meet the right person. You think you'll only date a man who has a full head of hair, and then the love of your life is almost bald; you won't consider a woman with children, then you find that you adore her little boy almost as much as you adore her. You won't believe this until it actually happens, so by all means set up your wish list, but don't be surprised if the non-negotiable factors are the ones to go. The magical, special something that you're waiting for may come in an unexpected package.

## 7. Practical Considerations

When it comes to dating through agencies, the Internet or personal ads, it's essential to establish some guidelines for selecting the people you're willing to meet. Otherwise, the range is just too wide and the choice too bewildering. Here are a few questions to get you started. Don't worry about finding the perfect answers – you may wish to adjust your search criteria later, once you've had some experience of proactive dating.

This might sound like a shopping list, and after all you're looking for love, not a business arrangement. But you're only making conscious a process that goes on anyway. If you meet someone at a party you'll be applying just the same kind of assessments. How old is he? Does he live nearby? What's his job? Proactive dating means considering all these factors in an honest and upfront way, rather as village matchmakers used to do. You're being your own matchmaker, so you might as well enjoy the role.

- How far will you travel to meet someone? You may be mobile, but bear in mind that if you offer to drive from Cornwall to Aberdeen, it could be hard to arrange follow-up dates.

- What age difference will you consider? Be realistic, especially if you are looking for a partner to go forward in life with.

- What part might health play? Are you looking for someone with the same level of energy or fitness as yourself, or would you consider getting involved with someone who has a serious disability or a progressive illness?

- What financial status would you expect in your partner? Are you willing to support him or her if needs be?

- What kind of profession and education are you looking for in someone you meet? Guidelines are best here, not dogmatic requirements.

## Stephanie's Criteria

Before Stephanie met Martin on a walking holiday, she dated through an online introduction agency and newspaper ads. She thought about the requirements she had specified then:

*I was possibly too limited about how far I was prepared to travel. As for age, I was looking for someone within about eight years either way. I always feel they should know something about the pop songs you like!*

Politics are also important to her.

*I'd be quite reluctant to meet anyone who was a Tory! That was one thing I asked Martin when we met: what newspaper do you read? And I'd be very reluctant to go out with someone who wasn't as bright as I am. It wouldn't last. Martin is very well read.*

Of course, the criteria will be different for everyone, and you will only get to test them out when you start meeting new people. But if they are authentic to begin with, reflecting the real you, then it will be easy to adjust them later as experience shows you the way.

Congratulations! Now that you've defined your key aims and intentions, you've done a lot of the preparation for launching a purposeful relationship quest. You're ready to test the water. In the following three chapters we'll give suggestions on how to launch your search. Where do you look? How does this whole proactive dating thing actually work?

CHAPTER THREE

# *Your Search: Ready to Start, But Where to Look?*

The good news is that it is now much easier to meet new people than it was 20 or even 10 years ago, by using the Internet, ads and agencies. Taking an active approach to finding a partner has become widely recognized and accepted across all age groups. New websites and personal columns are springing up all the time, and gone are the days when one was considered a sad loner for browsing through the personal ads. But although you may be *lol* ('laughing out loud' in cyberspeak), when you find out just how many opportunities there are, you still need a route map to navigate your way through the landscape. Each method of proactive dating has its pleasures and its pitfalls, and we recommend not only our guidelines to help you, but finding a dating buddy or two along the way to support and encourage you.

You may start to go on blind dates, but don't date blindly. You've already prepared the ground in working out your aims, and now it's a question of how to implement them. Hold the two poles of your quest in your mind: love and practicality. If you can embrace both the idea of true and lasting love, and that of taking practical measures to find it, you have actually encompassed the essence of the quest, and this will help you to be kind to yourself, to meet others willingly, and to go forward towards fulfilment.

In the next two chapters we will go into the process of using Internet dating, newspaper ads and introduction agencies in more detail. This chapter gives you an overview of the different lines of approach, and suggests how to manage the resources that will help you: the dating budget, the dating friend, and your personal appearance and well being. We also encourage you to open up your sexual potential, especially if it has been dormant for some time.

## Avenues for Proactive Dating

Choosing the path to take in looking for a partner needs reflection. Which approach will suit you best? How much time can you devote to it? Thinking about dating is one thing, whereas starting your search is quite another, just as dreaming about a house feels very different to actually putting your house on the market and buying a new one.

Here are the main routes you can take to find a relationship. You might choose to try more than one at once, or to try different ones in succession. We advise being moderate in the amount that you commit yourself to at first, until you've experienced what level of time, emotion and energy each one will require. Time and patience may be needed, so pace yourself accordingly.

### Internet Dating Sites

These are websites that contain the profiles of people looking for a relationship. You can either put up your own profile, or respond to those already on the site. To use an Internet dating site effectively, you need to have basic computing skills and regular access to a computer connected to the Internet.

You can enter most sites just to have a look, and see samples of profiles and photographs of members, but you will need to pay a subscription if you want to use the full service. This varies from site to site but usually includes the facility to exchange emails with other members.

Internet dating is a growing culture; it's a way of life for the younger age group, and fast being taken up by the over-40s. As the sites multiply it's especially important to find ones that suit you, with enough members of suitable age and interests. You may have to go through a process of trial and error before you find the sites that you like and feel comfortable using. There are specialist sites too, catering for particular interests, age groups or religious faiths. Searching the Internet, picking up tips from magazines and talking to your friends can be a good way of discovering new sites.

You'll be able to protect your privacy as no one will know your personal email or home address, and you can use a pseudonym online if you like. You don't have to post a photo of yourself on the site, though you will often get better results if you do.

Internet dating has the advantage of being something you can do from home initially, without the immediate need to make phone calls or meet up, and you can survey a wide range of people before beginning real-life dates. The usual approach is for one person to email the other and, if both are interested, to exchange a few emails before agreeing to talk on the phone or meet up. The disadvantage is that a number of those signed up to the site will simply be trying it out for fun; some are looking only for sex, some conceal the fact that they are married and a few, unfortunately, are fantasists who create a fictitious persona online.

But don't be put off by these factors: Internet dating sites have plenty of genuine and interesting people using them. They are a relatively easy place to start your search. Among our interviewees, Adrian and Valerie, Jessica and Evan, and Hannah and Hugh formed successful partnerships through Internet dating.

In terms of skills, you will need simple computing ability to search the Internet, navigate around a website, send an email and upload a digital photograph.

## Personal Ads

These appear in both local and national newspapers, and in various magazines and journals. The sections have names like 'Kindred Spirits' or 'Encounters', and the ads are printed as classifieds, with brief descriptions and headings that attempt to be eye-catching on a crowded page. The pages are divided up into male and female ads, and it's relatively simple to pick out possible candidates by age and location. Many have a good number of advertisers in the 40–65+ age group. If you are interested in an ad, you can call to listen to the person's voice message, where they talk about themselves in more detail.

It's usually free to place ads, but listening to voice messages, including those in reply to your own ad, is through a premium phone line, and charges can mount up quickly this way.

There is a greater degree of security in the printed ads,

as opposed to the Internet, as advertisers have to lodge their details with the publishers. Placing a personal ad also involves a slightly higher degree of forethought and commitment, so that people advertising are more likely to be genuinely looking for a relationship.

Getting started is easy. Once you have picked out some ads that you like, you can listen to the voice messages that go with them and, if you're still interested, leave a message of your own, so that the person can call you back for a chat. Depending on the distance between you, arranging to meet usually happens quite quickly after the initial phone call, if it's going to happen at all.

Ads don't have the advantage of photographs, but you can tell a lot about a person by their voice. You can always arrange to swap photos by email or post before you meet.

It's worth surveying several different papers or journals, to find out which personal ad pages you prefer. This may be partly determined by the publication's readership. If you like an alternative lifestyle, you won't find your soulmate so easily in a conservative newspaper, and vice versa. However, it is also dependent on how well the facility is run, since a good personal section gains a reputation and people of all outlooks will use it if they know it's reliable. There is nothing to stop you advertising, or responding to ads, in more than one publication, or trying out different ones in succession.

Of our contributors, Stephanie, Claudia, Lara and Cherry found genuine relationships through newspaper personal ads. Martin had plenty of responses to his ad, but then he met Stephanie on holiday.

## Introduction Agencies

These are run as a personal service to introduce clients to each other, on the grounds of potential compatibility. If you are interested in joining, most agencies of any worth will interview you in depth first, and if you join, they will prepare a profile for you which you can approve or amend. Their job is to try and match you with someone of similar interests, in the general age group and location that you've specified, and they can take other factors into account that may be important to you, such as education, profession, lifestyle and so on. You will be given profiles of other members to look at, which can be followed up by a phone call and perhaps a meeting.

A plus feature is that everyone who signs up to an agency parts with good money, and is therefore serious about wanting to meet a partner, or whatever level of relationship they have specified. It can be very expensive, several hundred pounds at least, and represents a significant financial commitment on your part. But this can give you a sense of security, along with the knowledge that the agency is taking your quest seriously, and working on your behalf.

However, the agency is only as good as the people on its books, and not every profile you'll receive is likely to be a winner. The pool of members is much smaller, in general, than that of a newspaper or Internet site, so it may not be possible to meet all your criteria. Most agencies also have far more available women than men. The agency limits its involvement to introductions, and though there may be a little bit of hand-holding to steer you through first dates, once you have met someone you would like to see more of, it's up to you.

Some agencies have different grades of membership, ranging from a more basic, computerized search, to dedicated 'head hunting'. They may also offer social events, mixers for their members, and the facility to search for a companion rather than a partner if you wish. They do sometimes have an upper age limit for their books, but increasingly these days agencies are more realistic, and know that there is a burgeoning market for the 45+ age group. Some even have members in their 80s.

Two of our couples, Anthony and Claudia, and Kate and Douglas, met in this way.

## Speed Dating

You sign up for an evening event in your area, and talk to a person of the opposite sex for about three minutes at a time. All the men and women meet up in turn, and you mark your card with an indication of whether you'd like to see any of these people again. The organizers will then arrange to pass on this information, and likewise to let you know if there is any response towards your charms. However, you will need to search hard to find speed-dating events for the over-40s, let alone the over-50s. At the moment, it's largely a young person's game, even though it has appeal as a lively evening out and a chance to meet others face to face without any commitment or (in theory) awkwardness. Perhaps speed dating (or maybe slow dating?) will develop for a mature and discerning clientele in the near future.

## Dining, Social and Activity Clubs

If you prefer to meet people through shared activity and social interaction, then this could be the way forward for you. Regional and local newspapers and magazines can be a good source of information on singles organizations and events.

Many towns and areas have dining clubs, some of which are franchised nationwide. The format varies from an evening meal in a restaurant, to which any members may turn up, to carefully planned dinner dates to which three or four selected members of each gender are invited. Dining clubs are sometimes non-profit-making, with just a modest joining fee and the cost of the meal to reckon with, or they may be commercial enterprises that require a more substantial investment.

Social clubs for singles vary widely, from local organizations to networked clubs that may have a branch in your area. Kate joined one around the time she became interested in meeting someone: 'It's quite nice to have arranged walks, meals in pubs. It's ideal for someone like myself who has a busy week. You don't always want to be spending the weekend with your married friends.' But check out the age range they cater for, and what kind of event is on offer before you turn up eager and bright-eyed in your best party gear. A serious discussion about current affairs might not be to your taste if you're hoping for a lively drinking evening.

Activity clubs offer the chance to try out anything from rock-climbing to bird-watching or ballroom dancing. 'Spice', a major organization with branches throughout the UK, charges a quarterly membership fee, and has a separate charge for each activity that you choose. There are day, evening and weekend events, both locally and nationwide. Members are of all ages, and although it is not a singles club, the organizers admit that a high proportion of its members are in the 'hoping to meet' category.

## Travelling

Organized holidays can be a great way to meet people, and you might even find a partner, as Stephanie and Martin did when they went on a walking holiday. Another couple we know also paired up on a walking tour, as they shared good wine under a starlit Tuscan sky. Small group holidays are often very sociable; you can go with a friend or on your own, as there are usually plenty of solo travellers on these trips. There are also travel companies which deal specifically with singles holidays, though they may not guarantee an equal number of both sexes. Other companies may forgo the usual 'single supplement' as a special deal on certain holidays, which will both be easier on your pocket and attract others who are going it alone.

Cruises are popular with a broad range of people, and each cruise usually includes a significant number of single passengers. As a newspaper article on cruises puts it: 'The social diary at sea offers a wealth of ways for single travellers to find cruising companions' (*Daily Telegraph*, 21st July 2007). The cost of travelling alone can be high, though, as ships often only offer double cabins, although some are now being re-fitted to accommodate more single berths. There are mixer events for solo passengers, and it's easy to talk to other people at meals, on excursions, or at onboard events. Cherry met Robert on a cruise; they were both shipboard lecturers, sat next to each other at dinner on the first night, and never looked back.

## Introductions from Friends

Don't overlook this as a possible way to meet a new partner, but make sure that your friends know that you're looking. Especially in midlife, friends and acquaintances can assume that you are quite happy in your single state – they may even envy you. It does no harm to open their eyes to your wishes, and to let them know, as quietly and discreetly as you like, that you wouldn't mind being introduced to any eligible single people of their acquaintance. Be careful, however, of friends who try and project-manage your re-entry into the dating and social arena; take charge of your own search, while using resources around you wisely to help with this. Your friends are part of your social resources.

## The Dating Buddy

It's invaluable to have at least one friend who will be your dating buddy. Ideally this is someone who has tried out proactive dating, who knows something about the procedure and the pitfalls you may encounter. It's someone to laugh with when you share your funny story of the disastrous date, or hand you a tissue if a potential new romance gets nipped in the bud. It's a friend who will encourage you to take the first steps, and to keep trying if your courage runs out. And the same friend will be delighted for you when you find love again, and say, 'I knew it would happen!' If nobody springs to mind who can do this, try asking among your friends and acquaintances. You may be surprised how many of them have walked this road; even those now in partnerships may have used the Internet or the ads a few years ago.

You need your dating buddies because not everyone understands the point of searching for love. Although there is a strong move towards proactive dating in general, there are still pockets of resistance out there. It's not uncommon to find certain friends staring at you in horror if you announce that you're dating through the ads or Internet. They assume that you will only meet losers, conmen and gold-diggers, that's if you survive the inevitable rape and mugging on a first date. And then, of course, there is the impropriety of taking such a step. Claudia had a few friends who could not cope with the idea that she was meeting men this way. 'They think, "It's not the way to go, it's not the right order of things – if you don't meet someone in more natural ways, you're just not meant to meet."' Even now that she and Anthony are married, she hasn't enlightened these friends about the introduction agency. 'They think we met by chance!'

It took Jessica four years of proactive dating before she met Evan: 'There were several times I gave up, but my friend Suzanna encouraged me each time I faltered. She had to really push me back into dating just before I met Evan because I was convinced by that point that it was hopeless.'

## How Cherry Became a Dating Friend

*I was having lunch with Charlotte, an old school friend. Charlotte had never married, but she had a daughter who had recently left home for university, and was now freer to follow her own path. She seemed exceptionally keen to see me that day, and I wasn't sure why. We talked about our children, work and other former classmates, but I felt that there was something else on her mind that she couldn't quite bring herself to speak about.*

*In between the Thai fish cakes and dessert, she suddenly gained courage. Leaning towards me, she whispered, 'I want to know how to do it. This dating thing. You've been trying it out, haven't you?'*

*Charlotte had been reading personal ads in the paper, but was bemused by the process.*

'What do you do with those box number things?' she asked me.

'Well, you tap it in when you've phoned through to the site, and then you listen to the person's voice message. You can just listen – you don't have to leave a reply.'

This was a revelation to her. 'So he doesn't know that I've rung?'

'Not if you don't want him to. But why not put your own ad in? That way, the men are courting you, and you can just choose whom to ring back after you've listened to their messages.'

I knew Charlotte was nervous and might give up at the first hurdle, so I decided to suggest an approach that could help her to keep going if success didn't come quickly.

'Think of it as a project. Something you're going to put energy into and have fun with, but not pin all your hopes on. I think it's better to be in touch with several men at first. Listen to their voice ads, have a chat on the phone, and decide who might be worth meeting up with.'

Charlotte drooped. 'I suppose I'm afraid of the rejection. I don't know if I could take it. Maybe this is not the way for me.'

As Charlotte has a real talent for the written word, but is a shy person, I wondered if the personal ads in the paper were the right place for her to start.

'Why don't you have a look on the Internet sites, where you can read the profiles that men have put up and see their photographs? You might find it easier to start with emailing, rather than talking on the phone.'

'But how am I going to put up a photo? I don't know how to do it,' she wailed. 'I could ask my daughter, but I don't want her knowing. Or anyone else for that matter.'

Never mind the technicalities at this point, which aren't difficult anyway. I wanted to inspire her to join the unofficial society of midlife daters.

*'Lots of people are doing it. It isn't shameful. How else do you meet new people at this age? The younger generation take it for granted now. Okay, so you might prefer to keep your daughter well away from your love life, and she probably doesn't want you in hers, but it's not such a terrible thing if other people know about it. We need to be proactive if we are to have any chance of finding a new relationship.'*

*I could see this was breaking new ground, as she mused thoughtfully.*

*'I'll be your dating friend,' I said. 'I had dating mentors who really helped me with the process and gave me the courage to do it.'*

*'Thanks,' she said. 'I'll think about it. I really will.'*

## Dating Advice from our Interviewees

The people we interviewed are also keen to help you in your search. Their advice is to get out there and be proactive, but to safeguard your well being en route.

**Stephanie:** *Go for it! Life's too short.*

**Kate:** *You can't sit at home waiting for that person to come to you. You do have to go out and try and meet them in whatever ways that you feel that you can.*

**Adrian:** *It's not enough to assume that the right person will just turn up – you also have to do your bit.*

**Anthony:** *Definitely go the proactive route. Any other route is less reliable.*

**Hannah:** *You can use any means to find somebody, but the key for me was defining what I wanted.*

*Claudia: Do try it out, but don't think that if it doesn't work for you at first that it's because you are lacking in any kind of way. You have to be careful not to let your own self-esteem get knocked.*

*Dawn: Give it a go, but don't think every person you meet is going to be 'the one'. Really try and see if you like them as a person, and don't be taken in by the trappings they may have.*

## The Budget

*Claudia: It's going to cost you, whatever you do!*

Even if you do not like to say the words 'love' and 'money' in the same breath, you will need to think about your financial resources when you begin your search for a relationship. Proactive dating is an investment. Plan for it, budget for it, and spend your money with a good grace.

### *The Late-night Spender*

You've been sitting at the computer for hours, working your way through the same few Internet dating sites, looking at the same old faces coming up. You're tired, and somewhat dispirited. Definitely time to go to bed now. Ah, but why not just take a quick glance at that other site your friend told you about? Mmm, some interesting profiles here. New hope floods in; maybe if you subscribe, then at last you'll be on track to meeting the right person. You reach for your credit card – STOP! Have you budgeted for this? Have you thought it through carefully? The site will still be there in the morning, and probably in six months' time too. Tomorrow, review your budget. If there's money to spare, take a closer look at the site in the cool light of day, and then make an informed choice.

Believe us, we write this from experience.

## A Practical Approach

When you go on holiday, you check how much it's likely to cost you, and whether it represents good value for money. Proactive dating is no different; a crucial part of a well-organised campaign is planning your budget, since you need to spend money to meet new people. Although money doesn't equate with love, using your financial resources carefully helps to put your search on a steady footing and may also help to see you through the inevitable highs and lows of the quest. It can take time, so, ideally, plan a budget that you can sustain over a lengthy period if necessary.

You know yourself well enough to figure out whether you tend to be penny-pinching, extravagant or relatively even-handed with your money. Few of us strike a perfect balance. Decide whether you need to unclench your tight financial grip a little, or to rein in your ever-optimistic, perhaps misguided spending patterns. Budgeting, even in a flexible way, will help to give you confidence out there in the field.

Anthony had been a businessman as well as a mariner before he retired, and this stood him in good stead when he met Claudia via an introduction agency. He knew that he wanted to achieve his aim as fast and effectively as possible, and he wasn't afraid to spend money to do so.

'In business, I learned that if you want anything, you must pay for it,' he says. Although he knew, of course, that love can't be bought, nevertheless he felt that paying for professionals to help him in his search was essential, and the better the service he paid for, the better value he would get. He bought into a premium service offered by a quality agency. Result! It was only a few months before they sent him Claudia's profile, and he would certainly recommend others to make the same investment. 'To think that you might meet someone by chance is just pie in the sky.'

## Setting a Budget

A good starting point is to plan how much you are willing to spend over the next year in the search for a new relationship. Here are the most typical kinds of expenses that you may need to cover.

### Direct Expenses

- **Subscriptions to Internet Dating Sites**

Typically, these run at around £20 a month, and become cheaper if you subscribe for longer periods. Bear in mind that you may want to change sites after a month or two and look at a different range of profiles. You can join some sites for free, but this usually gives only limited opportunities for emailing contacts or seeing photographs.

- **Premium Rate Phone Calls for Personal Ads**

Most newspapers allow you to place a personal ad for free, but to listen to your replies (usually) and to listen to other people's ads (always) there's a premium-rate fee. Even a modest use of this service can cause your phone bill to shoot up by about £40 a month. If you allow for a reasonable expense for phone calls, you won't get a nasty shock when the bill comes in.

• ***Subscriptions to Introduction or Dating Agencies***
Joining an agency is a major step, as it means parting with a significant sum of money. Fees can run from around £400 for normal membership to £1,000 or more if you choose a dedicated search service. Be aware that initial interviews can also cost money (£50 is normal).

## *Indirect Expenses*

These are the kind of expenses that you might incur in meeting new people. It may not be essential for you to budget for these, but it can be a boost to your confidence to allocate special resources to them. Here are some of the possible expenses that we have thought of. You may come up with other ideas too:

- new clothes
- a good haircut, hair colouring or re-style
- beauty and health treatments
- cosmetics
- travelling to dates
- money spent on dates, for meals, entertainment, etc.
- joining a supper club, singles club or solos holiday
- phone bills and/or Internet accounts for increased chats and emails
- flowers, food, décor for anticipated home visits
- new bed linen for closer encounters.

### Reviewing Your Budget

As you're going along it's a good idea to check out how the budget you have set suits your needs. You might wish to make adjustments to it. However, our main advice remains to do so only after some consideration, not because you have just read an article about an excellent introduction agency or want to fill an empty evening listening to voice ads.

### Second Phase, Third Phase

If you don't find a significant relationship in the first phase of proactive dating, or if a new relationship fails to consolidate (it happens), you may need to launch your budget all over again. That's one good reason why it's important not to overspend first time round. And if you've budgeted well and wisely, you're far more likely to say, 'Ah well, better luck next time.' Changing your tactics and starting to plan again can be fun, and re-infuse you with the spirit of adventure that you need on your journey.

## New Start, New You

*Valerie: I put a lot of energy into getting fit, getting slim before I came to meet Adrian the first time. I put a lot of effort into my clothes and haircut.*

*Martin: My late wife said to me before she died, 'You must marry again,' which was a generous thing to say. She also said, 'In order to be attractive to another woman, you must lose some weight!' I did lose two stone after her death, partly because I couldn't be bothered with cooking. When you lose weight, though, you feel more attractive anyway.*

Love can surprise you. When you have committed to wanting to find love, it may be waiting for you just around the corner. Whether you have had a string of dates or are only just beginning your search, love will play its own game of timing, and can spring up before your eyes at any moment. So, as the old Boy Scout motto says, 'Be prepared.'

If you follow the steps we suggested in the last chapter by preparing the way for the search, you are already at an advantage. Focusing your intention brings renewed energy, the search for love inspires enthusiasm, and a decision to manage your quest wisely will help to create presence, that indefinable something which strengthens your being and draws other people to you. So as soon as you begin the relationship search, you have a chance to step into a new, more vibrant and more attractive version of yourself.

Aim to look and feel at your best when you set out on your quest. We don't suggest going to extreme lengths, such as having plastic surgery or dressing half your age. The success of your search depends upon your essential self, the authentic you that someone else can love for a lifetime, not glitzy appearances that bear little relation to your real personality. But this doesn't mean obscuring your sexuality or wearing dowdy clothes on the premise that the other person should love you for who you are, like a kind of test in a fairytale. This is real life, and first impressions count for a lot. You can be sexy and enhance what you have without going to extremes.

Work from the inside out, but don't neglect the outer you. Enhance what you have. Going about it can be fun, and will boost your confidence.

## Presentation

Here are some suggestions for improving your appearance and well being, and maximizing your appeal. (Men, this section is for you too! We know that hairdos and fashion are more of a female province, but a good makeover can do wonders for a man as well. You'll be able to work out your own version of our recommendations.)

- *New clothes.* Throw out some of your old ones first, which will motivate you to update your image. Look through some style magazines, browse the clothes rails in shops, and maybe take a friend to help you on your buying spree. Good clothes in the 'smart-casual' category may be more use to you for first and follow-up dates; save the ballgowns and tuxes till later. New underwear is a must; it might be on view sooner than you think, and in any case it will make you feel sexy and alluring.

- *Hairstyle.* Have a good look in the mirror and see if it's time for a change to something more contemporary, or a different colour or style. If you have stayed with the same hairdresser for years out of habit and you think they won't want to work with you to change your look, ask around for a recommendation to a new star stylist, and treat yourself to a really good cut.

- *Fitness, weight and energy.* Most of us know, deep down, if we need to make improvements in this area. But make them gently and safely. Go for more walks – you will look livelier and healthier. Try out salsa classes, yoga, Pilates, tennis or enjoyable activities rather than opting for punishing exercise regimes if you hate the gym. Limit portions of food on the plate, and refuse second helpings; buy good, organic fruit and vegetables, and try out new recipes for healthy food. Anything that promotes your general good health will boost your energy and enhance your attractiveness, two big pluses for dating.

   • *Hygiene and grooming.* We may have slipped into somewhat sloppier routines in our single state, which won't bear too close scrutiny. Sorry to mention this, but have you reviewed your habits of showering, underarm shaving and leg waxing, use of deodorant, teeth cleaning and breath freshening, hair washing and nail trimming? Indulge yourself in lovely bath oils, body rubs and, if possible, treat yourself to a couple of spa sessions which will do wonders for your skin as well as leaving you with a great sense of well being.

## Sexual Renewal

By midlife, practically everyone will have had many years of sexual experience, and so, in theory at least, it's the aspect we need the least guidance on when contemplating a new relationship. Many people find that sex can be even more fulfilling at this age. The power and passion of sex, the warmth and tenderness of physical caresses can all be a wonderful part of relationships in middle and later life. You already know what you like, how to give and receive pleasure, how to go with the urgency and how to linger over the gentler moments of contact. Or do you? Maybe our sexuality can also go through a process of renewal at this stage of life. Maybe you got married several decades ago when oral sex, for instance, was still somewhat taboo and, being satisfied with what you already had with your partner, you never got round to exploring it. Or maybe you always wanted to find out about new positions, erogenous zones and Tantric techniques of prolonging sex, but felt self-conscious about trying all this out.

So it pays to take a fresh look at your own sexuality at around the time you get interested in dating again. You might want to buy a book or two on sex to expand your horizons. Read younger style magazines to find out what other people are getting up to – or say they are getting up to! If you haven't chatted to your friends about sex for years because you were in a settled relationship, take a deep breath and have a go. This is not about feeling obliged to get up to every trick in the book, but about enjoying your own sexuality and being ready to respond to a more adventurous sexual relationship, if it appeals to you. Preparing yourself now can make you more relaxed and confident when you find yourself in a close embrace again, and more ready to choose whether to go with it or not, rather than reacting from old patterns and preconceptions.

We hope that you're now feeling confident and attractive, and that you're ready to discover all the interesting people out there who would like to meet you. It's a whole new country to explore, and in the next couple of chapters we'll be guiding you through some of the different ways of contacting them. If you have taken your time to think about the approaches we've suggested so far, and have prepared yourself in these different ways, both physically and emotionally, you will be in very good shape to navigate these new pathways. A new, sparkling and alluring you is launched into the world. Enjoy!

# CHAPTER FOUR

# Internet Dating

Internet dating has really taken off in the past few years, and has become a popular way to meet new people. Almost half the couples we interviewed had met each other through Internet dating sites. These people tended to be at the younger end of our age spectrum, in their 40s and early 50s, probably because that age group has been more accustomed to using computers and to making new contacts online through work. But this situation is rapidly changing and many people in their 50s, 60s and older are now Internet-savvy. Saga, an organization for the over-50s, recently relaunched its social networking site, correctly analysing that the desire among that age group for socializing online is growing fast.

Even though Internet dating has become fairly widely accepted and is no longer considered the province of hapless people who can't get a date any other way, there are nonetheless several hazards involved, not least of which is the potential for deceit. We'll look at the downsides further on in this chapter, and go through the various ways you can protect yourself and ensure as positive an experience as possible when meeting people this way.

There is a plethora of dating sites now, and choosing which ones to use can seem daunting. In this chapter we're going to look at how to pick the right site for you, how to write your profile and present yourself, how to choose whom to get in contact with, and how to manage the early stages of communication before you actually meet.

## How Online Dating Works

So what does online dating involve, and how do you actually do it? The easiest way to get the lay of the land is to go and visit a few of the more longstanding sites such as Match.com or Guardian Soulmates (dating.guardian.co.uk).

Most of the sites will let you look around and see how the site works and what sort of people have put their profiles there, before you sign up. This helps you have the confidence that it will be worth your while to write a profile and upload a photo.

Some sites will only let you look at the profiles of a few people before you sign up, which doesn't make a lot of sense as a policy. You're much more likely to buy a subscription if you see someone you like. That's certainly what happened for Adrian and Valerie. They met through dharmamatch.com, a specialist site for people with spiritual inclinations.

*Adrian: I found Valerie on the site before I was a registered member. So I had to sign up and make a profile. Seeing Valerie's profile made me want to pay the money. There was no doubt in my mind that I wanted to get in touch with her. She just sounded really sincere and authentic and warm and humorous, and just a really good person.*

Unlike Dharmamatch, many of the sites are huge, with thousands of members. Guardian Soulmates has 80,000 members (as of January 2008) and is growing all the time. Obviously the advantage of a big site is the element of choice. With so many people to choose from, you'll be more likely to find someone you like. On the other hand, with so many people on a site, trying to find the one who would suit you can feel like looking for a needle in a haystack. On a specialist site you know you have something in common with many of the people there, and a smaller number of profiles to read through.

What many people end up doing is to register on two or three sites, with a mixture of a huge site and one or two smaller specialist ones. Of course, if there is a site that seems to have lots of your kind of people on it, then that one site may well be enough for you.

Often, people who are actively looking for a partner will put a profile on two or three sites, so don't be surprised if you start seeing the same familiar faces each time you check out a new site.

## The Profile

So what had Valerie written in her profile that made Adrian want to sign up on the site and immediately contact her?

*Valerie: Well, obviously you want to put yourself in a positive light. I wanted to say what I was like, and what I wanted. I said I was a strong independent person but just now and then I want to be looked after and given a hug and some flowers and asked how my day went. And you do that, don't you? [to Adrian] That was what you signed up for.*

## Setting Up Your Profile

Each dating site has its own questionnaire for you to fill out, which will make up your profile. Some of these are very long, and some are simpler. Remember, you don't have to answer all the questions, some of which may seem silly or intrusive to you. You don't have to reveal your income or financial status, for example, even though most of the sites try to get some information on this.

There is always space to write something about what is really important to you and what you are looking for in a partner. So write something heartfelt that is real and will give the reader some sense of who you are. It can be quite brief, as long as it is individual. There's no point writing something bland and generic like 'I am a nice person who likes to cuddle in front of the fire and walk hand-in-hand along the beach.' Be specific. Also, remember that most people primarily respond to the photo, and may be put off by too long a profile.

To sign up for some sites, like Parship (the dating site for *The Independent* newspaper) and eharmony.com (a large American-based site), you have to fill out a lengthy questionnaire which can take several hours to complete and supposedly will enable the site to match you to the right partner.

The problem with this method, and the matching programmes on other sites, is that it takes little account of the Jack Sprat element in partnership: we don't necessarily want to be with someone who is a carbon copy of ourselves.

It's good to allow for the possibility of being pleasantly surprised by your next partner. Maybe they have an interest or a skill you have not encountered before but which would open up your horizons. Allowing for some serendipity and keeping an open mind can help your life to expand positively. So don't write so exclusive and rigid a shopping list of qualities that it precludes potential mates from contacting you.

The shopping list is itself a problem. It's all too easy for the section under 'What are you looking for?' to become a long list of idealized qualities. Again, just as we suggested when it comes to describing yourself, try to be specific and not generic, and leave some space for the unexpected.

## Other People's Profiles

What can you really tell about someone from reading his or her profile? Well, if you read it carefully, you can find out an awful lot. None of us is perfect, but some of us are more suited to relationships than others.

If the profile is too brief the person probably isn't serious, or has great difficulty expressing themselves. If it's too long they may be over-fond of the sound of their own voice, and perhaps suffer from self-importance. Or they may lack confidence and be trying very hard to please. If the profile is too full of demands about how you must be (gorgeous, always happy, low-maintenance, etc.), then the person may be too picky and critical to make a good partner.

There are some things that really should raise a red flag. Anyone who talks only about fun, with no mention of any other aspect of relationship, is likely to be either superficial or terrified of real emotion. Be cautious with anyone who mentions alcohol more than once. Anyone who uses half their profile space to talk about how much they hate negativity and can't bear angry people is probably suppressing rather a lot of anger themselves, and may not be resilient when it comes to the ups and downs of life. Any long list of pet hates is reason not to get too enthusiastic about the person. Anyone who talks only about what you can do for them is probably a taker.

Men can be very good at writing funny profiles. Women can be funny too, but our research showed that it was more often men who would write a really amusing profile. While wit is a very attractive trait, being funny isn't enough on its own for most of us, and sometimes people use humour as a cover-up for emotional issues that could be a problem later. That said, a funny profile will attract a lot of responses, and that gives you more chance of meeting someone you really like.

Overall, if you can do it authentically, a balance of wit and seriousness is the best style to aim for. You will find further suggestions about constructing a profile in the next chapter, in the context of setting up ads in the newspapers.

## The Midlife Profile

While there are some gender differences here, there are many aspects of describing a partner shared by both genders in midlife. Everyone, pretty much, is looking for someone who is enthusiastic about life and good fun. The word 'play' comes up a lot in ads, and it's clear that, by midlife, many people are finding that adult life is overly serious and they are looking for a companion to balance out the chores of responsibility. They may have come out of previous relationships bruised by criticism and discord, feeling that being in a relationship has been hurtful and that they have not been encouraged to be themselves, or sufficiently understood.

The gender differences between ads tell us a good deal about what elements of relationship and the opposite gender men and women have found difficult in the past. Men's ads tell us that many of them fantasize about meeting a woman who is 'still a girl' and 'doesn't take herself too seriously'. She is 'slim, with a waist', 'low-maintenance' and 'fun-loving'. One can easily speculate that these are men coming out of a marriage with children in which they felt harassed by responsibility and a wife worn down by domestic drudgery and exhaustion. It is easy to criticize these ads as being shallow, but it is also important to realize that for men, just like women, relationship is a source of emotional nourishment, and that this includes fun and lightness.

Women rarely mention physical appearance (other than to object to beards) and speak a lot more about emotional qualities. When describing the man they are looking for, the most common words women use are 'gentle', 'kind', 'funny' and 'empathetic'. They don't want workaholics: they want attention. They speak about men who are tender, affectionate and emotionally available. This suggests that women in midlife are often suffering from previous experiences with men who were not developed in the feeling realm and who put their own interests – work, sports, nights out with the boys – before the feelings of their partner.

Men, on the surface at least, are looking for a female version of themselves: sporty, slim, with not too much going on emotionally. Women are looking for a male version of themselves: caring and empathetic, and not going to give anyone a hard time about the physical realities of ageing.

But ... we have to remember that this is what people say they want. In reality, what people actually want is both more simple and more complex. More simple in that what people write in their ads is often their best-case dream scenario, and most of them would be very willing to dump much of it in exchange for the pleasure of a warm body next to them in bed and a good-natured companion to share life with. More complex in that we don't fall in love entirely from the conscious mind. The unconscious has a lot to do with attraction, and despite what the ads say, many men are drawn to strong, bossy women, and women to solemn, moody men with beards.

So think carefully about what you say you want in your profile. Take other people's requirements seriously, but with the awareness that they may be describing an ideal they would be happy to let go of in exchange for the joy of being with you. You may still be right for each other even if there is an aspect that doesn't seem to fit at first glance.

## Photos

The photo is the most important element in your profile. It's a visual shortcut that gives a ton of information, some of it consciously absorbed and some of it subliminal. All the dating sites emphasize that people with photos get many more replies than those without.

Photos give us a hint of whether we will be sexually attracted to someone, although because sexual attraction actually happens primarily through pheromones, we can't really know if there is physical chemistry until we actually meet up.

The most obvious reasons for someone not having a photo are either that they are not at all photogenic or that they want to keep their online activities a secret, if, for example, they are married and looking for either an escape hatch or someone on the side.

But this is not necessarily the case, and it is worth your while to look at the profiles of people without photos: some people feel they can't put up a photo because they have a public occupation that might be adversely affected by publicity. Some may be shy, or may not want to be recognized by people who know them.

Some of the sites have evolved to help those who have a job or position that makes having a photograph on a public site not such a good idea. On Guardian Soulmates, for example, you can choose to restrict views of your photograph to people you allow to view it, whose profiles you have already read and who have expressed an interest in you, so you have some control and maintain some privacy. On Parship, photographs are only visible to fully paid-up subscribers.

If there is no photo available and you like what someone has written in their profile, you can always ask them to send you a photo via email.

## Your Photo

For your own photo, use a very recent colour photograph in which your eyes are open and looking at the camera. No sunglasses! It's best if you are smiling, as most people look better with a smile on their face and it invites the looker to smile back, and thus want to get in touch.

Looking friendly and approachable wins out over looking aloof or in a state of airbrushed perfection. This is about finding a partner for an intimate relationship, not an ad in a glossy magazine.

The photo should show you to advantage, but not be an actual lie. Using an old photo is a bad idea, however good a picture it is and however much you are sure you don't look any different now. The most authentic you will shine through in the most contemporary photograph. You want someone to be attracted to you now, not you ten years ago.

Beware of showing too much flesh. Women showing a lot of cleavage will attract men who are looking for sex only, and not a full relationship. Men with their shirt off just look desperate, however great the body.

Above all, don't use a photo that clearly has your partner cut out of it, or worse, shows you with your arm around another person, even if it is your child. If it's an ex, it implies you're still involved with them in your mind, and if it's a child it implies they'll be coming on the first date. Just use a nice, clear photo of you on your own.

Photos with distracting background information don't work well. People look pretty much the same with sunglasses and a ski jacket on, shot from a distance. That slightly grainy photo of you at a party with a glass in your hand isn't such a great idea either. And don't be wearing a business suit and sitting at a desk: you'll come over like a workaholic who has no life.

A head shot is the best photo to show your personality, and gives the most emotional information. It will work best if you have a genuine smile and if the photo is in focus and well-lit.

## Age

A lot of people lie about their age on dating sites. If there is a discrepancy between the life story and the age, or between the photo and the age, by all means ask questions. One man told Lara that he felt he had lost five years from his life due to grief, and this justified him shaving five years off. Another said, 'But everyone says I look younger than my age, and I get on really well with younger women.' Please!

It is, of course, all too easy to lie on the Internet. But it's not a good idea. If the relationship works out, you will have to come clean eventually, and your new partner might not take the deception lightly. Lying about your age will also distort your dating process: people will not be getting an authentic version of you, and so you'll attract the wrong ones. It sends everything off-kilter, so best to be honest.

There are age cutoffs, and once you're over 50 you may well get somewhat fewer approaches. It's true that if you say you are younger than you are, you are going to get more attention. But while it might be flattering in the short term to get a zillion emails from younger people, in reality they are looking for someone closer to their own age and it's unlikely your correspondence is going to lead you into a workable relationship.

Whatever your age, being truthful is the best policy. We know many examples of people in their 60s who were honest about their age and attracted suitable responses because of their photo and what they said about themselves. Annette, a 65-year-old American living in France, recently met Jean-Luc, who is 69, through the big European Internet site, Meetic.com:

*He's everything I've been looking for. Like me, he's a horse rider who lives in the country, and we're already discussing me moving to live with him in Normandy. Being older is not the issue when it comes to finding a partner – it's finding the right person that makes all the difference. If I had lied about my age he wouldn't have been so interested in me, because he wanted to meet a woman close to his own age who was ready to live an active but retired lifestyle.*

## The Costs

Dating online will cost you in terms of both time and money. It is all too easy to spend hours trawling through the sites looking for Mr or Ms Right, and exchanging chatty emails can also take up long periods of time. Then there is the financial cost of becoming a subscriber with full benefits such as online chat and unlimited emails.

These costs will affect your choice of how many sites you sign up with, and which ones you choose. More than two or three will begin to have a big impact on your life both in terms of the time it takes up and the amount of money it costs you. It's usually better to decide on one or two, with a maximum of two or three, and concentrate your efforts there.

## Time

Once you've set up your profile and uploaded your photo, it's a good idea to think about how much time you have to spare for browsing the profiles of potential mates and for exchanging emails. It can be tempting, especially after a long period of being single, to spend hours on the sites – at least you're getting some kind of attention, and it begins to feel possible that love might re-enter your life.

But spending excessive time online can unbalance your life and therefore unbalance you, and make it more likely you will become a little obsessive and make poor choices as a result. Don't let the rest of your life fall apart because of the often illusory promises of Internet romance.

There is no need to answer every email with a lengthy missive in which you bare your heart and soul. In fact, you don't even have to answer every email at all. Just as you wouldn't necessarily get into a conversation with every person who eyed you up as you walked down the street, you don't need to respond to the kinds of emails that only say 'Nice profile' or 'Just thought I'd say hello.' It's not worth it, unless of course you like the person's profile and decide to 'just say hello' back.

Often the people who write such emails are outside your preferred age range or other clearly stated parameters, and they are just seeing if you are prepared to stretch those. If you really feel clear that you don't want a relationship with a big age gap, or to date someone who is not yet divorced, or who smokes sometimes and drinks every night, then stick to your guns.

At the beginning it can all get quite overwhelming, especially if you have a nice photo. Women often receive a great many responses when they first get into a site, but many of these will be from men who are not serious about a real relationship. Give yourself time to weed these guys out. Men also often receive a barrage of welcoming emails, which can be very flattering, but take your time to sift through the profiles and decide who you would like to contact.

### Money

Most sites encourage you to set up a profile for free. Then the sites vary somewhat in terms of what you can do before taking out a subscription. Sometimes you can reply to emails without a subscription, but you can't be the one to initiate contact. Online instant chat only operates if you are a subscriber. Most of the sites charge you less the longer a subscription you take out. Charges are around £20–23 for a month, levelling off to the equivalent of £10–12 a month if you sign up for six months. At Guardian Soulmates you can sign up for three days initially for a small amount of money, and at Match.com you can have three days of full membership for free, to see how you like the site.

## Security

In the worst-case scenario, dating online could compromise your personal security. But with common sense you can ensure your personal safety as much as in any normal day-to-day encounter.

The well-run sites use email checks to make sure you are using a bona fide email address, and won't let you into the system until they have verified this. Then you are at least trackable through your email address, which gives information about your location. Once you sign up for a subscription, they have even more personal details about you.

But you also have to do your own checking. Asking questions is the best way to make sure someone is who they say they are. These days many people can be found through Google, so you can do a search for the person there. If you have any doubts, or if they are reluctant to divulge personal information, back off from contact. Be particularly careful if you are in contact with someone in another country, as their identity may be harder to verify. And, of course, never send money to anyone you haven't met or don't know well, however plausible their story appears to be.

The vast majority of people dating online are completely genuine, and there is no reason to be afraid. But you do need to be sensible.

## Early Stages

All those people on the Internet looking for love. Whom do you contact? Are you overwhelmed by the choice?

Often women find when they register with a new site that they get several, sometimes many, emails from interested men. If you've been feeling a lack of male interest for a long time, this can be intoxicating. All those men who want to write to you, talk to you, go out with you! But first, you have to do a reality check. Some of these men will be married or otherwise partnered up. Some of them will be only interested in playing around and in having a virtual relationship.

And for men, suddenly there are tons of available women right there on your computer screen! Who do you make contact with? What are your criteria? Sometimes men make the mistake of firing off emails to every woman they find remotely attractive. Step back, breathe deeply, and take things more slowly. Don't just be seduced by a pretty photograph or catchy tag line. Read what they say in their profile properly. Would you really suit each other?

For everyone, it's wise to take your time. Don't be rushed by the lure of romance. Listen to your body and your inner knowing. It's worth trying to figure out whether a profile has been put up by someone who is looking for a sexual encounter, as opposed to a full relationship. This isn't always easy to be sure of, but there's not much point in following through on people who aren't looking for the same thing as you. Online names like Slowhand or Funlover suggest that sex is the prime motivation. If you want a long-term relationship, look for someone whose name and profile show that they are looking for the same thing.

At the other end of the spectrum there are people who fall in love with a photo and profile and decide this is the person for them before they have even met up. Lara had several experiences with men becoming infatuated with her before meeting:

*It can be very seductive when a man immediately forms an attachment to you and begins emailing you and then phoning you every day and talking about the future. I found it flattering and it appealed to the romantic dreamer in me. If the man seemed genuinely a possibility for me in terms of his interests, I found myself hoping that this was the one, and a couple of times began to form an attachment in my own mind. But when men were so keen so early, I found that there was always some real problem in the background. It was usually that they had only just broken up with their previous partner and were on the rebound, desperate to assuage their emotional pain by falling in love straight away. Their instant attachment to me was a dream, but not reality.*

It's only when you meet up that the connection becomes grounded in all the senses. So in the early stages of Internet dating, keep your feet on the ground until the first meeting. If you really like each other in person, that's the time to begin to let yourself dream about a romantic future together, and not before.

## Internet Dating Dead-ends

- People who just want an email relationship.

- Married people or those who are already involved in a committed relationship, looking for something on the side.

- Younger people looking for a sugar daddy or experienced woman.

- Someone who doesn't give you their phone number or doesn't want to know yours after a few emails.

- Someone who has been on the site for years and is always dating multiple people.

## *Separated But Not Divorced*

You may not want to exclude people who are separated pending divorce, but be careful. While this category can work out, given enough time, beware if you find they talk about their not-quite-ex all the time. Sometimes couples do get back together.

Sometimes people begin dating before they are ready, which can at best hinder and at worst completely mess up a budding relationship. If you do meet and like someone who is in the midst of a divorce process, it is usually a good idea to hang fire and keep seeing other people. Once their separation is complete, and if you haven't met anyone in the meantime, you can see if there is still mutual interest in a long-term relationship.

## Making Contact

If you like the look and impression of someone's profile, then get in touch! After all, that's what you signed up for. Many sites have pre-email, testing-the-water features to allow you, in effect, to look across a crowded room and see if there is any response back from the other person before you commit to walking across and introducing yourself.

These features include the wink or smile, but in our experience these are not always effective. If someone wants to contact you, it feels much better if they go to the trouble of writing a short, personal email. A wink feels like a wink in real life: trivial and maybe even insulting to some people. A smile can work a little better, but is still all too easily ignored. If you want to make an impression, then write an email.

Many sites have a feature where you can make someone your favourite. Mostly how it works is that one person makes another a favourite, who then responds in kind. Then the initiator feels confident to send an email. This seems to work quite well.

## Who Should Make First Contact?

It's often said that women like to be contacted, and that men prefer to initiate contact. This may be true, but if you are a woman looking for a man on a site don't let this stop you from introducing yourself if you see the profile of someone you find attractive. Especially on the big sites, he might have missed seeing your profile.

## People You Should Not Contact

It can be disheartening when you compose a carefully worded profile and put up a good picture, to find that you get emails like this:

*with such a looks how come u r single ???*

*i tell u – if u r passing by Leeds just let me know*

*u wont be disappointed ...*

These brief emails in text-speak are usually from people who are just trawling for sex or entertainment. In the case of the Internet, it's not rude to ignore certain kinds of approaches. You may be tempted to send a polite response, such as 'Thank you for writing, but I don't think we have very much in common. I wish you very good luck in your search for love,' or similar. But the Internet is not a social occasion at which mutual notions of politeness operate. If you get a juvenile and abrupt first email from someone, in all likelihood if you respond all that will happen is that you will get an angry reply, along the lines of 'Who the f*** do you think you are?'

It is often best not to respond to emails that are brief and impersonal. If the person can't take the time to introduce themselves pleasantly, they are unlikely to be someone you want to know.

Now, of course, if the person has written to you nicely and yet you still think there is no reason to pursue contact, by all means write back in the same tone. They will usually thank you for being clear and for letting them know how you feel so that they don't waste time waiting for you to respond.

Know what you are looking for. If you know you want marriage, don't waste your time with people who say they just want some fun. There's usually a place to say what kind of a relationship you're looking for, and if someone has ticked 'have some fun', and not 'long-term relationship', why waste your time?

## The First Email

*Valerie: I had given up. I'd had my profile on two or three sites – one for single parents and another one I've forgotten now, bigger and more general ones. I'd had my profile on those sites for several months. I'd started off really curious, but after you've seen hundreds of profiles of people you don't want to connect with you go off the whole thing. I hadn't had any messages I wanted to reply to. Men replying to 50 women at once, really illiterate, in text-speak. Nothing that attracted me at all.*

*I thought, 'I'm never going to meet anyone like this.' So I took my profile off the larger ones but I left it on Dharmamatch because it was a smaller site and I wasn't getting any replies so I just didn't bother. One day, I was supposed to be doing some work and I was procrastinating and so I went to look at my email, and there was a lovely long letter from Adrian. He said some really complimentary things.*

***Adrian:*** *I decided I was really going to try and write a letter that couldn't be ignored. I had a really strong feeling just from the profile that if she was available I really wanted to get to know her.*

***Valerie:*** *It had a strong effect on me, so I went to look at his profile and I thought, 'Oh, he looks really nice.' And my sister came over and looked at the profile too, and she said, 'Yes, you've found a good one there.' The letter was very personal to me, not a general letter. He mentioned the points of contact from things I'd talked about in my profile, the books I'd mentioned that he had read.*

This shows the importance of the first email. Don't make it too long, but do show that you have really read the other person's profile. Do share something about yourself that isn't in your profile, but not your whole life history. End with a question that will encourage the other person to write back to you.

Beware of getting caught up in an intense email exchange too soon. If it all starts to feel too much, just back off. It's a good rule of thumb to allow 24 hours to go by between emails, especially at the beginning.

## Relating Through Email

Valerie says: 'Straight away we were emailing every day. It was very warm right from the beginning.'

When you click with someone, it's amazing how much you can sense intuitively, and the email relationship can get very close very quickly. This has advantages and disadvantages.

The main advantage is that you have the opportunity to make a connection with someone you otherwise would not have met. Maybe they live on the other side of the country, or in a different country entirely. The disadvantage is that, until you meet, you can't be sure how much of this connection is real and how much is wishful thinking.

Then there's online chat, which can be great fun and provide lots of information, allowing you to get to ask and respond to questions in real time. But in most cases you'd be much better served by a phone call. Just move the whole thing along so you don't waste time with someone who won't work, and speed up meeting the person who will.

With Instant Messaging and webcams, people can get pretty intimate in a virtual context before they even meet. But this can have negative repercussions. We recommend that you don't get too intimate too soon, and certainly not before you have actually met the person. If it turns out that they are not at all like they said they were, or that you feel no chemistry in person, it will be embarrassing to turn them down after you've already had a virtual kind of intimacy. More crucially (because we all have to get beyond embarrassment to do online dating in the first place), you may feel that you have to go through with becoming lovers with them, as if you already have made some kind of commitment. Putting the cart before the horse can get you into trouble, and also adds a huge weight to the first meeting: instead of meeting in a friendly, inquiring way, you are meeting with a big romantic expectation looming over the whole thing. This is great if it works out, but can also scupper a relationship which might have led to a real connection if it had been entered into a little more judiciously.

This is why it's not a good idea to stay at the email level for too long. Given human nature, a prolonged email relationship with someone you think you fancy will start to get sexual, even if only a little bit, and you will be creating a fake relationship based more on fantasy than on reality. If you like each other, pretty soon you need to talk on the phone. If you like the sound of each other, move towards arranging a meeting.

Valerie says: 'One day my computer started going weird and I was worried it was going to crash, so I emailed him my phone number. It was a good excuse …'

## Talking on the Phone

Making the transition from email to phone is actually quite a big step in Internet dating. It's one thing to write emails to someone you only know as a picture on your computer screen, and quite another to speak to a real person on the phone. It's the moment at which the imagination begins to ground in reality.

Try to keep an open mind at this stage and resist the temptation to become too attached too quickly. A flurry of friendly and engaging emails doesn't necessarily mean you are going to like what you hear in that first phone call. It may be that the man you thought had a very sexy photo turns out to have a squeaky voice, or you find that the woman you thought looked gently seductive has what to you sounds like a harsh cackling laugh. It can also go the other way – you can fall in love with someone's voice before you meet them, and this can also be a mistake.

Those caveats aside, we get a huge amount of information through the voice – it tells us a great deal about someone's emotional temperament. And how well they listen to you in the phone call speaks volumes about their ability to relate.

## The First Phone Call

When do you make the first phone call? Timing needs vary with this, but for people who are genuinely interested in creating a real relationship, you will feel like having phone contact within a week or so, say after three or four back-and-forth email exchanges. (There's more information about the first phone call in Chapter 7.)

Don't fall into the trap of having too many phone calls before you meet in person. This is just as bad as too many emails. You can build up a lot of intimacy over the phone, but remember, you still don't know what this person really looks like, what they smell like, what it feels like to be in their presence. There's a great inclination to be wearing rose-coloured spectacles – you so much want this to work out, especially when you first begin proactive dating. Then after a few bad experiences of meeting people who are ten years older than their photographs (and not as tall, with a lot less hair, or 20 pounds overweight when they said they were slim), you can become cynical and not even want to bother.

These two extremes of being over-optimistic or jaded are the twin evils of online dating, the pendulum swing that can really get in the way of success.

## Arranging the First Meeting

If you like someone, try to meet up fairly soon. Adrian and Valerie met three weeks after their first email exchange, which is a sensible amount of time. Long enough to feel confident that you really would like to meet the person, yet not so long that you have formed too great an attachment and already decided this is the one-and-only.

*Adrian: Because she's from the area near where my mum lives, when I was next going to visit my mum I wrote Valerie an email and said, 'How would you like to meet?' Thinking she'd say, 'Oh, that would be nice.' But then I got this reply which was backing off, saying, 'I'm not sure I've got the time, I've got this and that on.'*

*Valerie: Which was due to complete panic on my part. I'd been with my ex-husband since I was 16, and went to an all-girls grammar school and had no experience of dating. I went completely back into 16-year-old mode. And my friends were all saying be really careful.*

*Adrian: I couldn't quite figure out why she was suddenly withdrawing and I thought, 'I'm not going to stand for this, I'm not taking no for an answer at this stage,' so a couple of days later I phoned her up. We had a nice warm conversation, so I asked her again if I could see her the next week.*

**Valerie:** *It was easier after I had heard his voice. And it was nice to be asked again. I suppose you just get a better sense of someone if you've spoken to them as well as written.*

**Adrian:** *You can hear a lot from the voice, it carries a lot. Whereas you can perhaps manufacture more in email. Although the kind of communication we had been having, I don't think you could manufacture that.*

**Valerie:** *Yes, but you have to remember I didn't have anything to compare it with.*

## Creating a Sustainable Strategy for Online Dating

- Sign up to two or three sites max. Choose them with care.

- You don't need to answer every email.

- If you get a lot of responses, don't let all the attention go to your head, including all those charming emails from people young enough to be your children.

- Don't waste time or energy on people who aren't serious about finding a relationship, or serious about wanting to get to know the real you.

- Do check out what the person really wants. Read their profile carefully.

- Take your time. Don't be rushed by people who are pushing for rapid exchanges of email early on.

- Talk on the phone reasonably soon. That way you won't waste time with someone whom you realize isn't right for you once you speak with them.

- Same goes for meeting up: try to meet within a month of the first contact. Extended phone relationships can be a waste of time and energy.

- Understand that there will be ups and downs of feeling: of expectation and disappointment. Try not to buy into the extremes. Maintain a reasonably even keel.

- Be persistent and patient. Don't let disappointments knock you back.

- Allow for serendipity, and trust in your destiny. There's an element of fate in whom you meet, whether on the Internet or off.

Internet dating works, there's no doubt about it. It's a creative use of modern technology that keeps on growing and developing. No doubt by the time you read this there will be new additions to the ways in which we can use computers to find potential partners, but in this chapter we've covered all the basics. No matter how sophisticated the technology becomes and how many more websites appear, the central issues will still be the same and this information will help you navigate the world of online dating with skill.

Next we're going to investigate personal ads, an older but still very popular method of meeting new people and finding romance.

# CHAPTER FIVE
## *Ads and Agencies*

The first personal ad was placed in 1727 by one Helen Morrison, who announced in the *Manchester Weekly Journal* that she would like to meet a gentleman to spend time with. Unfortunately for Ms Morrison, this was considered so shocking that she was sent to the lunatic asylum for four weeks to correct her moral values!

Luckily for us, things have moved on. Personal ads are now booming, along with introduction agencies, though they too had a rocky start and were initially considered to be no better than an organized form of prostitution.

In this chapter we look at both ads and agencies, and this, combined with the information about Internet dating in the previous chapter, will give you an excellent grounding in dating resources. At present it may feel rather like that first driving lesson, sitting behind the wheel of a stationary car while the instructor drones on about easing in the clutch and never ignoring the oil warning light, and you on the other hand are simply longing to hit the road. But please bear with us – by the end of this chapter you will be conversant with all the main methods of dating, and be able to make your choices confidently.

The first, and longer, section of this chapter focuses on personal ads, and the second on introduction agencies. However, even if you prefer one route rather than the other, we suggest that you read both sections, as both contain key issues. Bear in mind, too, that ads and agencies are changing and indeed improving their services all the time. You'll need to do some of your own research to see what's available, and to supplement the information given here. Our aim is to supply you with the necessary tools so that you can make the best of the current resources out there.

## The Notebook

First of all, treat yourself to a new notebook. Pick one that you'll enjoy writing in. It can be as bright and frivolous or as soberly professional as you like. Your notebook will become a fascinating record of the people whose messages you listen to, who you talk to on the phone, and those who you eventually meet up with. Writing notes will help you to remember their details, to pick up a conversation where you left off, and to feel more secure in your selection process. After your first phone conversation, you may think that all the details are embedded in your memory for ever, but when you have had around 20 of these, and listened to twice that number of messages, you'll be likely to muddle up names, ages and professions.

*Cherry: I placed personal ads intermittently for two to three years. Going through my faithful notebook, I find that I had nearly 70 voice messages left for me during that time. I made phone calls to about 50 men in response, and met about 20 of them. Looking through these notes now I can actually remember everyone I spoke to. So it's not at all cold-blooded to keep records – in fact, it has the opposite effect, and has kept the experience alive for me in a very human way. Even now I feel some warmth and affection towards those I spoke to – well, most of them, at least!*

You can also keep notes on different publications and agencies that you may be researching, about the clientele they cater for and how they work. If you place an ad, you will also need to remember pin or box numbers, and the different phone lines for retrieving messages or asking for advice. Your notebook is an ideal place to store these.

## Personal Ads

### Newspapers and Magazines

Many of the national newspapers in the UK have well-established sections of personal ads which appear once a week, including *The Daily Telegraph* (Friday), *The Guardian* (Saturday, repeated Sunday in its sister paper *The Observer*), *The Sunday Times* (Sunday), and *The Independent* (Saturday). Some also link up with online dating sites, but all can be operated entirely by reading the newsprint and using the telephone, without the need to go on the Internet. Local newspapers often carry ads too, though be aware that these may be syndicated with other regional papers. Some publications run ads for particular categories: one West Country newspaper has a section called 'The Farmer Wants a Wife', for instance, and *Saga* magazine runs ads for the over-50s.

Browse the publications that you like and ask your friends if they can recommend any particular ones. Try your favourite newspaper, as the readership is likely to have the same social and cultural orientation as you. Have a look at local magazines too, including the 'What's On?' type, and any journals that cater for your professional or leisure interests. More and more are starting a personal ads section, and even highbrow publications such as the *London Review of Books* may include one. (Where there's a lack, you could always suggest it to the editor. It does, after all, make money for them.)

## How to Choose

To find a publication that's suitable to start with, ask:

- What are its outlook and readership?

- Are there enough people in my age group advertising?

- What is the general tone of the advertisements? Are they straightforward, funny or clever, and does that fit with my style?

- Do the ads seem sincere?

- Are they orientated more towards looking for relationships, or could they just be for sex seekers?

- Do any of the ads appeal to me – would I be interested in talking to any of the people on the page?

- How is the section operated? Does it look straightforward, and are the charges set out clearly?

## Costs

It is nearly always free to advertise. The publishers make their money by charging premium phone rates that stack up at around

£1 a minute when you listen or respond to the voice message that goes with an ad, or to the messages that are left for you when you place an ad. Naturally it's up to you to decide how many messages you want to listen to, but even a modest amount of listening and responding can raise your phone bill by £40 or more in a month.

**Hot tip:** Get familiar with the telephone keypad shortcuts on each site, which often allow you to skip preliminary announcements or to move on to the end of the advertiser's voice message, thus saving valuable minutes.

## How Do the Ads Work?

The publications do a good job of making placing and responding to ads as straightforward as possible; you'll find printed details of the phone numbers that you need to use, and how much this costs. When you use their services, there are clear automated instructions to follow, and usually a live helpline for further advice. Security is excellent, and no one else can discover your phone number, or access messages left for you.

The nuts and bolts of placing and responding to ads given here are guidelines only; check with your chosen dating page for the exact procedures.

## Placing an Ad

You are usually asked to write a short ad (around 25 words) for the printed page, and to record a voice profile over the phone, giving more details about yourself. You'll also need to leave some personal ID details, which remain confidential. Once the ad is published, interested readers can listen to your message, and leave messages for you, which you retrieve by phone (premium rate again). You can sometimes arrange to have text alerts to let you know when there is a new message waiting – you need to pick up messages promptly, as they will be deleted after a while. Your ad may well be repeated for several issues, but you should be able to withdraw it or alter it during this time if necessary.

## Listening and Responding to an Ad

Call the number given, enter the box number that goes with the chosen ad and, after you've listened to the voice profile, you can leave a message if you like. At this point you'll need to give a phone number if you want to get a reply. Some advertisers try to insist on all callers leaving a landline number only: 'Ladies, we have to start off on a basis of trust. I will only respond to your landline number, never to a mobile,' proclaimed one misguided advertiser, but how can there possibly be complete trust between two people who have never met? Most safety guidelines recommend that women leave a mobile number only in the first instance. For a man to leave a landline number, on the other hand, can be a good idea, giving a woman confidence that he is genuine and available.

## The Pros and Cons of Personal Ads

- You can begin discreetly, in your own time, from your own home. (This also applies to Internet dating.)

- The safeguards are usually greater than on the Internet, as more personal identification is required and it takes a greater degree of commitment to place and respond to ads.

- It's more selective, but also more restricted, than the Internet, in terms of the type and number of people advertising.

- You don't have the advantage of seeing photographs immediately, though some personal ad columns are now including facilities to send photos to your phone or email.

- You have the opportunity to hear someone's voice, and can tell a great deal about them from this.

- The initial process may be slower – you have to wait at least a week or two before an ad is published – but once you begin to pick up messages it's generally quick to move to a live chat on the phone, and to a date if you wish.

- It's manageable. You remain in control of choosing how much or how little you use the services, and it is relatively inexpensive.

## *But I Don't Want to Advertise Myself!*

Once you have got to grips with the practical elements of personal ads, you may still find that you have reservations about using them. Shades of Helen Morrison still haunt the land, and many of us feel a frisson of fear about entering what was previously a no-go zone. The 40+ generation has not grown up with the idea that normal, bright, attractive people can or need to use such a public means to find love, and for some of us it's a very new way of looking at the world. But in seeking a new relationship, we are in any case stepping into the unknown. The first move towards change has already been taken, so why not follow it through?

If you are a woman, you may feel that placing an ad could expose you too much. But this is a well-protected and discreet approach, and your friends and neighbours will know nothing about it unless you tell them. If you are a man, you might feel that it undermines your pride as a go-getting male. Claudia's son, Jethro, is an attractive man in his 40s who works in the film industry and has plenty of beautiful women to choose from. But he hasn't yet found that special person whose outlook really complements his own. Claudia encourages him to try the personal ads or join an agency, but so far he refuses to contemplate it. 'Oh God, no, I can't. If I go down that route I'll think I've really failed.' She believes that he's missing the point.

By advertising, you are simply announcing your presence to those in a similar position who are also looking for a relationship. In essence, is it any different to how we indicate socially, at a party for instance, that we're single? In proactive dating you are simply making a natural process more conscious and deliberate. Accept your intention to find a relationship as a worthy aim, as it's important to the integrity and power of your search. Pride and fear should not be confused with a sense of true self-worth and the power of discrimination; you may have to jettison the first pair in order to progress, but never the second. And being older and wiser gives you a distinct advantage in this respect: experience and knowing what you want count for a lot.

### Should I Place My Own Ad, or Respond to Other People's?

If you are a woman, there is a lot to be said for placing your own ad. 'Men advertising are inundated with replies, so it's best to put in your own ad, and then you can screen the respondents' (Claudia). Her argument has a point, since once a woman has placed an ad, she can then sit back and wait – hopefully – for the replies to roll in. It boosts confidence to find messages in your voicemail, rather than hanging around to see if the man you left a message for will ring you back.

In the basic courtship process, studies show that in almost every case a woman puts out the signals, then waits to receive attention from the male in return, capably screening out any unwanted advances. This goes well with the idea of a woman placing her own ad. A man, however, usually prefers to move in the direction that he's chosen for himself. So he is often happier responding to an ad, as it gives him the chance to pursue a woman he likes the sound of. Juggling with responses to his own ads can, by contrast, sometimes be confusing as a man would often like to please them all! Colin, a likeable doctor in his early 50s with a warm telephone manner, found himself absolutely inundated with replies to his newspaper ad. Each time he dialled in, another clutch of messages was waiting for him from women the length and breadth of the country. After meeting a few of these women, he panicked at the choice available and withdrew from the process completely.

## Making a Balanced Choice

Ultimately, it's a matter of personal choice as to whether you place the ad or answer other people's. It does help to understand our basic, instinctual drives, though. And although we may be sophisticated and mature, living in an era of gender awareness and equality, it is still basic sexual attraction that drives us towards searching for a mate, whatever our age. You will also always need to take your personal preferences and circumstances into account. The ads pages would be very restricted if everyone followed the 'women advertise, men respond' rule.

'I didn't actually advertise, because I didn't know what to say,' said Stephanie, who found the process of constructing her own profile too daunting, and preferred to respond to ads which men had placed.

Sometimes there are very good personal or professional reasons not to put in your own ad; those working in the legal professions, those who are public figures or who are very wealthy, for instance, often need to be extremely careful.

Whichever route you choose, it's not set in stone, and you can easily switch from responding to advertising and vice versa, as you become acclimatized to the process.

## Placing Your Ad

This starts with composing a short written ad. It's your chance to make an impact, to describe yourself in an intriguing way. Being genuine does not mean being plain and boring. Read a couple of editions of the publication you'll be using, and see how other people are doing it. Some columns tend to be humorous while others are more romantic or matter of fact. You can either go with the flow or buck the trend. If everyone else is trying hard to be witty, then you might score a hit by going dreamily lyrical.

## Learning the Lingo

There is no shame if you need to get acquainted with the language of personal ads. A sophisticated television producer in his mid-60s, dating through the ads for the first time, confessed that it took him a while to work out what 'ltr' meant. (Long-term relationship, in case you were wondering.) Abbreviations are sometimes used to cram more words into the ad, so you might also see 'gsoh' (good sense of humour) 'ac/la' (all calls/ letters answered) 'iso' (in search of), 'ohac' (own house and car), 'wltm' (would like to meet), and even 'ntw' (no time wasters). Luckily, this is not the world of street rap or super-cool texting, so you'll be able to figure most of it out.

## Playing with Words

You can have fun with writing your ad. Practising beforehand will get you conversant with presenting yourself and expressing your personality in ways which will get your ad noticed.

Try the following:

1. Write a long list of all kinds of things that you like, however incidental: 'hot tubs, zebras, prawn sandwiches', for instance, and things that you dislike, such as 'moustaches, pineapples, polka dots'. You can use a few of these to sprinkle into your profile or ad to spice it up, and the list can, surprisingly enough, also help you to clarify what your real loves and interests are.

2. Pick out a few which have the same initial letter – e.g. 'cats and coconuts', 'mountaineering and Mozart' and see if you can find some pairings which might look good in an ad. You'll notice that other people are also using this device; it's effective, as long as you don't overdo it.

3. Try for a rhyming pair, but screen them carefully – 'history and mystery' (a little weighty), 'cars and bars'

(oh, please!), 'walks and talks' (better, but dull), 'spring and bling' (which is more entertaining), and so on. You might just find one that you can use.

Think of this as light-hearted mind gym, enjoyable homework that you can keep up in your notebook in idle moments.

## The Headline

The ads usually begin with a few words in bold type, and it is this headline that will catch someone's eye. So how do you want to appear on the page?

- Choose an opening word that has few or no competitors – there are too many 'Attractive' women and 'Professional' men advertising, for instance. Avoid overworked or ambivalent words such as 'bubbly' or 'assertive'.

- You could begin with your profession, if it's an obviously appealing one: among recent ads we looked at, the headline 'Fireman, 40,' followed by 'Attractive, dark-haired, deep blue eyes' certainly does something to a woman, whereas the bald pronouncement 'Dental Practitioner' was not an immediate turn-on.

- You can choose a song title, an allusion or a play on words if this appeals to you: Love is in the Air, Helen seeks Paris, Come Fly with Me, Knight in Rusty Armour, The Fuchsia is Ours (from a florist), Big Opportunity (from a larger woman) are some real-life examples. But beware: these can sound contrived or over-elaborate.

## The Ad

- Use the body of the ad to fill out the details about yourself. Try to give some genuine and useful information. People are pragmatic as well as romantic, and if you don't give enough clues they won't bother to spend the money ringing up to listen to your voice profile.

- Check the number of words you're allowed, and hone it until you get it down to length. Otherwise it may get edited for you, and you won't end up with what you want.

- Consider drafting in your friends or even your children to help. Yes, really – they can often name your best qualities and most interesting features with astonishing ease.

- Do include your age. 'Mid-50s' or '40-something' will do, if you prefer not to give it away exactly.

- Do include your region or town, so that someone will know whether you are within their area or not.

- Don't use suggestive words such as 'Fun-loving', 'Sexy', 'Exotic' or 'Uninhibited' unless you are game for anything. One woman who advertised herself as having 'the stamina of Champion the Wonder Horse' blushed for weeks afterwards as she listened to the replies she got!

- State one or two interests if you have room. Be practical in terms of selecting activities which you might share: travel, golf, photography, theatre all might appeal to either sex, whereas needlework, rugby and car maintenance don't have much pulling power. Don't mention things that everyone does, like watching TV, or that everyone likes, such as watching sunsets.

- Say what you are looking for: 'lively lady to share good times with', 'seeking that special person for ltr', 'tall kind man for friendship and maybe more' and so on.

- Include the age range of the person you are looking for. Men, please be realistic. You are unlikely to attract a genuine candidate if you request someone 20 years younger than yourself. Women, say now if you want to include an upper age limit, to avoid possible confusion and annoyance later on.

- You can add in something frivolous or funny to give your ad a lift: real-life examples are: 'Would like a balloon ride', 'Let's meet over a glass of champagne', 'Must love cakes and canals'. Check for possible blunders, like the man who unwittingly described himself as 'an old 60s swinger'.

- Most importantly, be yourself. Even though the printed ad is very short, try to convey something of your individuality and authenticity.

## Check Your Printed Ad

Do make sure that your ad is printed as you intended. Cherry found herself displayed under 'Men Seeking Women' (gender mix-ups quite often happen). We've spotted some real howlers, such as 'Knight Seeks Damson in Distress' and 'Seeking a Soil Mate'.

## *Your Voice Message*

'Being yourself on the voice message is the best way' (Claudia). The ad is a snippet, a glimpse that will attract people to listen to your message. This is your real opportunity to speak in your own voice and to convey your genuine personality and qualities.

You can speak for as long as you like, but a minute or two is usually enough. Less can be more, and in your desire to be sincere don't give out every detail about yourself. Save something till later, keep personal details about finances and old relationships private, although it's fine to mention that you're divorced, widowed or separated.

Most people will create a better message if they prepare what they are going to say in advance. 'Oh dear – oh, I don't know what to say!' is heard all too often on voice messages, and it's not particularly endearing. After all, someone is paying to listen to you. Write yourself some notes, but only write it out in full if you know that you can talk naturally this way. If it sounds as though you're reading from a script, it will come across as flat and rehearsed. But do practise your message, time it, and feel fluent before you actually record it for real.

Start with your first name (never include your surname), which defines you as a real person who wants to communicate with whoever is out there. Speak as if you are talking to an individual, that special man or woman who has been waiting to hear your voice and to learn more about you. Be friendly and warm, but not over-familiar.

Invite them to leave a message, and ask them to tell you something about themselves, including where they live and how old they are. These are facts that you'll need to know in order to decide whether to take it any further.

Remember that you certainly don't have to reply to every message that you get.

Don't worry – you can listen to what you've recorded and do it again if you're not satisfied.

## Leaving a message

The same thing applies if you're responding to someone else's ad: be as natural as you can, talk to the other person as an individual, and say something about who you are, including relevant details of age, location and interests. Don't ramble on for ten minutes; it's how you come across as much as what you say that catches the advertiser's attention and makes them want to call you back.

Avoid becoming a serial telephoner, who rings up dozens of people on the off-chance, and really try to connect with the individual you're leaving a message for. It's quite acceptable to ring up several people whose ads interest you, but don't do the carpet-bombing approach, responding to everyone of the opposite sex within a 40-year age range. One notorious caller rushed off his set piece to everyone: 'I'm Nigel, I'm genuine, considerate and caring. I don't like talking to machines, so do ring Nigel.' And then there was the drunken farmer, who rang a number of women but needed just a little more polish for his chat-up lines: 'My name is Johnson. If you ring and I'm out, just say Oxford (Aberdeen, Dawlish, Reading, or wherever you come from) and I'll remember which one you are.' Thanks a lot!

Then there was the professor who responded to Cherry's ad:

*He was Irish and had all the charm of the Emerald Isle, delivering this magnificent speech full of quotations from poetry, allusions to the beauties of nature and music, and an insistence that we should meet because we had so much in common. Delighted with his vocabulary, I called him up and we agreed to swap photos. I looked at his and thought him rather nondescript. He saw mine, and emailed immediately saying whoops, he hadn't thought this through, and he was really too busy at work to take anything on right now. A year later I advertised again, and got the same message, the same speech. So much for the personal touch!*

So be yourself, speak to the person as an individual, but don't overdo the chat-up lines. And although you want the listener to recognize you as a woman or a man, don't lay it on with a trowel; those who listen to ads often say that women come across as too winsome and girlish, and men as too boastful and assertive. Be a human being first and foremost!

## The Selection Process

Once you have listened to voice messages, either accompanying a printed ad or left in response to your own, it's time to choose who you'd like to single out and talk to directly. You may also need to acclimatize to this new experience. When you first discover all the people out there that you could meet, it can produce a certain feeling of euphoria, a sense of choice like being turned loose in a sweet shop. Allow yourself time to settle down: listen to messages again, even though it costs you. It's cheaper in the end than phoning everyone who might be an outside chance.

As human beings we do have a natural empathy with one another. Every person has an essence, a uniqueness that we respond to, and you may easily find yourself charmed by a voice profile even though the person could never be a match for you. Start as you mean to go on. This is dating, and you will need to reject more people than you encourage, which you would not normally do in social interactions. It may sound harsh, but if you encourage anyone you could only ever be friends with at best, you can cause offence and disappointment later on, and you can become entangled in an awkward way.

It's time to review your selection criteria again, but remember that individuals are not a list of tick boxes, and a certain amount of flexibility is needed. Allow some leeway, but keep your common sense. You may need to break some of your own search rules if the right person comes along, but don't throw them completely out of the window.

## Introduction Agencies

Anthony decided to join an introduction agency after he was widowed. He had one or two scary close encounters with women he already knew, who tried to move long-standing friendships with him into love affairs. He also had some unsuccessful forays into the local supermarket, after reading that this was where single men could meet their match. 'All I did was keep bumping into the church warden.' He recalculated his strategy; personal ads didn't appeal – 'too many bubbly blondes' – so he signed up with a reputable agency that covered his area of the country. It wasn't long, as we've discovered already, before he met Claudia.

## How to Choose an Agency

An agency will work on your behalf, selecting possible matches for you from their books, all from clients whom they have screened and interviewed. However, joining an agency means parting with a substantial amount of money, from around £300–400 up to several thousand for a dedicated search on your behalf. You may also have to pay an ongoing monthly membership fee. So this is not a decision to take lightly, and you owe it to yourself to make a careful choice. Check out which agencies cater for your age group; many more these days have woken up to the fact that there is a huge demand for finding a partner in midlife and beyond, and actively encourage this age range to come on to their books. Research the background of any agency that you're interested in; ask friends, request brochures and search the Internet for information about them. One agency in Gloucestershire made national news in 2007 when a disgruntled client sued them for giving her hopelessly inappropriate introductions.

There is a professional body, the Association of British Introduction Agencies (www.abia.org.uk), which regards itself as 'the authoritative voice of the introduction industry, with its members providing a reputable and ethical service'. Their website is worth perusing, and if you do choose to sign up with a member agency, you can be sure that they will follow the code of practice and give you a good service. However, bear in mind that there are also many genuine agencies who act independently.

Once you are considering an agency to join, you'll be

interviewed as a prospective client. The interview should be without obligation in terms of taking out membership, but you may have to pay for the interview itself (usually around £50, which will be offset against the joining fee) as this can take two or three hours, and may involve the agent in travelling some distance to meet you. Interviews take place in the client's home, in hotels or in the agent's office. You might wish to state a preference; Anthony wanted to see the offices the agency operated from, as part of checking them out, whereas Claudia felt more comfortable in her own surroundings. Your home expresses your personality, and it can be helpful for the agent to see this. There should be no pressure to part with any membership fees on the day: if there is, be careful, and if you are asked to pay in cash, don't proceed any further. Before the interview, do as much homework as you can, and after it, read the agency's literature carefully.

Interview the agency, just as they interview you.

- How many clients do they have on their books?

- How many are in your age range?

- What is the male/female balance of these? (It's normal to have more women than men registered, but much more than a 60/40 ratio will make things harder if you are a woman.)

- What grades of service do they offer, and what do these cost?

- Will they supply photographs for you to see? Some agencies don't offer these as a part of their standard membership, and you have to pay for a premium service to view photos.

- How many possible matches do they realistically have for you at the moment? This should be a well-thought-out reply, not just a glib figure of member numbers.

- How many introductions would your level of membership include, and on what basis? Sometimes the fee covers up to a certain number of introductions, and the agency may define this as exchanging a phone call with the person concerned, rather than a face-to-face meeting.

Other points to consider:

- Does the agent listen to you carefully, and do they respond to your questions? Beware of a set speech, at least after the introductory spiel, or of having your questions brushed aside.

- Do you feel in sympathy with the agent? An agent doesn't have to be a bosom pal – someone who is different in outlook to you can actually work very effectively on your behalf – but you should at least trust and respect them.

- Does the agency organize social events? This is a useful plus point, but not essential.

- Ask if you can see a sample profile.

- Will you have a chance to see and amend the profile they create for you?

- Think hard before parting with the fee. However good the agency, it's a gamble to enrol with them, and it's virtually impossible to get your money back if you're not satisfied.

## How Agents See It

Here is how one agent describes her work with clients. She has 800 people on her books (not all of whom are available at any one time), with an age range of 30–70+.

*When I meet a prospective client for the first time, I check their ID, verify their age, and encourage them to be realistic in their expectations. I don't accept everyone onto my books. I weed out obvious gold-diggers, and people whose requirements are too specific – someone who wants to meet a fellow horse-racing enthusiast, or who will only consider meeting a person who lives within ten minutes of their home.*

Her advice is tailored to the particular individual, and she doesn't give blanket predictions for success. She also warns them that, although she will do her best for each person, 'Chemistry is never predictable, and the service doesn't work well for everyone.' She charges for interviews, which can easily last a couple of hours. 'Otherwise, people treat it as a counselling service, and finish up by saying, "Thank you, you've made me feel so much better."' She takes photographs, prepares a draft profile, and asks for feedback on this before it's forwarded to anyone else on the agency's books. Once introductions are under way, she or her colleagues are on hand by phone to answer ongoing questions, or to give any back-up support needed.

## Profiles

Kate decided to join an agency. 'I thought I'd give it a whirl – I'd got nothing to lose.' After the interview, her profile was prepared for her approval and she waited with interest to see what would come through her letterbox in terms of likely matches. 'One or two were odd, one or two were okay.' Ultimately, however, the agency sent her profiles which were stretching possible compatibility to the limits – a ten-pin bowling champion, after Kate had declared an interest in sport, and a man who wanted to live in a Winnebago in Las Vegas after she mentioned her love of travel. Annoyed, she contacted the agency and told them not to send her anyone else unless they were really suitable. 'It took energy, it took time, and those were things I didn't have a lot of.' Luckily, the next person they sent was Douglas.

If you take out membership:

- Be realistic about the age of the people you will be matched with, usually within 5–10 years either side of your current age for both men and women.

- Be flexible about their professional status. A job title is only a label and isn't always representative of a person's personality, or their range of interests.

- Be prepared to meet at least one or two contenders. You won't know how well the agency is working on your behalf unless you do.

## Timescale and the Wheel of Fortune

If you join an agency, think of it as a long-term investment, as progress may be slow. Compared with the number of profiles put up on the Internet, and the ads in the paper, the membership of an agency is very limited, and you will usually only get to see one profile at a time. Our interviewees who met through agencies (Kate and Douglas, and Anthony and Claudia) consider that they were very lucky to find their partners this way. Their views on agencies in general vary, however. Kate began recommending the agency to her friends after meeting Douglas, only to find that they did not have the same success as she did. Anthony is positive about his decision to join an agency, and considers that the results were because he chose a quality service. Douglas feels that the agency sent him too many unsuitable candidates, but knows that they got it right big-time with Kate, and that this was the best avenue for him to meet new people. Claudia joined an agency after several years of using personal ads, hoping that fate would be on her side – and it was.

You are of course at liberty to continue with Internet or personal ad dating while on an agency's books, and it's probably a good idea to do so. Some agents have well-prepared horror stories of the dreadful things that can happen to you if you pursue your foolish path independently of them, but don't be deterred. Others actively encourage you, a good testimony to the belief they have in their own services and that they will do better on your behalf in the end. If you join an agency and then meet your partner through an ad or at a party after all, you may smile wryly in years to come when you remember the money that you spent on fees, but you won't regret it. Trying different avenues is all part of the journey, and it is the end result that matters.

Here is Kate's final advice on the subject:

*I do think that in this day and age, agencies provide a useful role in bringing people together. It's very difficult in your more mature years – you can't go to nightclubs. But fill your life with other things too – hobbies, meeting people, classes. Don't just be focused on an agency. If you're enjoying your life, however you meet people, they'll be more attracted and drawn to you if you're a happy person.*

Meeting people, in the end, is where it's at, and despite all the careful preparation, the phone calls and hours of scrutinizing profiles, it's only when you come face to face with someone that you will know whether you might be a match for each other. Now the real-life interaction begins, and romance may soon be in the air. But it doesn't mean throwing caution to the wind; having a strategy to manage your search from this point on is vital, as the next chapter shows.

CHAPTER SIX

# *Managing Your Strategy*

There is magic in meeting new people. Getting to know someone affirms that we are alive; looking into someone else's eyes, recognizing their individuality and essence mean that we are seen and known in turn. And when we move further into dating, perhaps a part of us that has been held back begins to open out to the world again. The heart unfreezes, and feelings that had been numbed by past experience thaw and start to respond to another person again. Even before love arises, the delicate nuances of emotion begin to show themselves, like the first colours in the sky heralding the dawn.

In the journey that you are now taking, be wise but not cynical. Looking for love while protecting yourself with a hard casing around your heart will only bring you into contact with other hard-bitten or uncaring individuals. Allowing yourself to open up gently, to be affected by someone else's presence, is part of welcoming love back into your life. There may be knocks and setbacks, and painful sensations may sometimes assail you, but if you can accept these as part of the process you will eventually find yourself liberated and renewed in spirit.

This is where having a good strategy comes in. The guidelines we suggest in this chapter, along with the wisdom and understanding you have gained over the years, will help you steer a steady course through the uneven terrain you're likely to travel through when you begin dating again. Be patient with yourself, and empathize with others who are also out there looking for human love and intimacy, however imperfect they may seem at times.

You are now beginning to make contact with new people by phone and email, and starting to meet them, and this chapter works as an overview, a plan of navigation for the journey. Its aim is to help you go forward with a good heart towards your destination. In later chapters we will be exploring the depth of feeling that can arise as new relationships are established, and the challenges and joys that these can bring.

First, we offer a dating strategy to help you to maintain your focus on your search, followed by some tips for staying centred, and then we look at the area of personal hopes and expectations, and how these can affect your progress. Gaining some clarity about these issues can help to clear your mind and keep your heart open as you enter the dating arena.

## An Eight-Point Dating Strategy

### 1. Date with Dignity

Be reassured that what you are doing is a perfectly sensible and practical way of finding a new partner. There are still people who do not understand this, or who cannot tolerate the idea of finding someone in a less than 'natural' way, but by now you probably know who your friends and supporters are in this respect. Remember that there are thousands of other people out there of a similar age who are doing just the same as you are in order to find love.

There are two keys to preserving your dignity: keeping a sense of humour and maintaining a degree of detachment. Both of these will help you to keep a mature perspective and retain your sense of self-worth while dating. But remember, too, that all the suggestions we make in this book are not absolute or rigid commands; as a wise adult, using your intuition, you will know when it's the moment to break the rules to find love.

**Claudia:** *I think a sense of humour is absolutely vital. The best way is to have a limited expectation. Don't go along to a meeting thinking that this is going to be it, or you're going to be disappointed nine times out of ten. You have to be very, very matter-of-fact about it.*

## 2. Try Different Approaches

By now you will have become familiar with the different contexts in which you can meet new people: Internet, personal ads, introduction agencies and activity, travel and social groups. Be ready to try another avenue if the first one you attempt doesn't suit you or has no effect. Try more than one at a time if you like, but we don't recommend taking on too much at once. Proactive dating does generate quite a lot of monitoring and admin, and you could get bogged down if you are fielding too many contacts at the same time. You can always try a different resource at a later date, if your search continues over a period.

## 3. Be Proud of Your Courage and Your Progress

As you begin to meet new people, look at your one-off dates and any short-term relationships as significant steps along the way. Even if you haven't yet found your long-term partner you are still achieving a great deal in terms of moving out of the single state. These chats and dates are indications that people want to meet you and to get to know you better. Keep faith with the idea that something real and long-lasting will eventually come your way.

## 4. Decide between Exclusivity and Multiple Dating

If you are meeting people through the route of ads and/or the Internet you are likely to have plenty of dates to choose from, and there is no ethical principle which says that you shouldn't meet as many people as you like. It's only a question of keeping a clear head and not using up all your stamina. But once you agree to see someone for a second date, you may wonder whether you should do this on an exclusive basis, and drop any other meetings for the time being.

We recommend you carry on with other dates until you are absolutely sure, rather than find later that you have spent several weeks or months on a connection that is going nowhere. If you cut out other prospective candidates too soon you may regret it if the hoped-for relationship doesn't gel. On the other hand, going out with several people at once can be confusing, not to say tiring, and may dissipate any genuine feelings that are building up for one person in particular. And of course there are cases where two people immediately know that they are right for one another, and there is no thought of continuing to meet others. Claudia recalls: 'The first time I saw Anthony and he smiled, that was it! It really was – it was like an electric current.'

Whatever you decide, it is important to be honest. People can have different expectations and assumptions, and you may need to spell out your intentions clearly. Try to find a tactful way, for instance, of letting the other person know if you are seeing other men or women at the same time. Give reassurance, too, that these are just friendly meetings, not sexual encounters – assuming that this is the case – and that therefore exclusivity isn't yet an issue. The other person may in fact welcome this news, as it takes the pressure off dating and avoids a hothouse situation building up in the delicate early stages of getting to know someone.

## 5. Monitor Your Energy

Dating is demanding. There is the effort that goes into sifting profiles and talking on the phone, plus the excitement and nerves of preparing to go and meet up for the first time. When you meet someone new you are using all your faculties: you are listening attentively and are observing and sensing everything that you can about them. You'll also be thinking of questions to ask them as well as fielding their questions about you. All early encounters involve considerable energy, and although a date may go well, you can find yourself tired, rather than exhilarated, at the end of it.

*Lara: When I first tried Internet dating I really had no idea what I was doing. I put up my profile, and immediately 50 men wanted to go out with me! This was more attention than I had had in ages, and I loved it. I picked the five I liked the best, and arranged dates with all of them in the coming week. Yes, that's right, I had five dates in five days. Complete insanity. Not surprisingly, none of them appealed and I dropped the whole project like a hot potato, exhausted from the attempt.*

So, take your time, allow enough time between dates to suit you, and resist the pressure to meet up again too quickly if you want to reflect on the meeting or to restore your own balance first. Keep tabs on your longer-term energy cycles too, and take a break from dating as and when necessary. You don't have to prove youthful stamina and impossible levels of energy. It's quite normal to involve yourself thoroughly in the process for six months or so, then to let it go for a few months while you catch up with other parts of your life. No one can sustain enthusiasm indefinitely, and it's better to have a break than to find yourself becoming cynical and world-weary – not a good state to be in if you hope to meet the love of your life. Give it a break, and then you'll usually find that you're raring to go again.

## 6. Take the Long-term View

It may take months or even years before you meet the right person. Include this possible timescale in your plans, and assume that you may go through one or two relationships before you find the one that will last. Jessica dated for four years before she met Evan. During this time she had several periods in which she didn't date, and then would go back for another round. Eventually, this persistent strategy paid off.

Although it may not always seem like it at the time, unsatisfactory relationships can help to prepare you for the real one when it comes, and to clear out old attitudes and hurts. When Martin met Stephanie he knew very quickly that she was the woman for him. It was 18 months after his wife had died, and he had met and dated other women in this time. The first contacts he made were all a part of the process, which also included reawakening to his own sexuality.

*So it was easier for me to say, 'Yes, that's what I want.' I wouldn't have been ready to respond to Stephanie if there hadn't been some history before it ... I suddenly realized that it was conceivable that I could be attractive again. When you've been married to the same woman for a long time, you don't actually know, when you're in a single situation again, whether you can be attractive to the opposite sex.*

Many people have a couple of short-term sexual relationships in the early days of searching for a new partner. These can be liberating, and useful in rebuilding sexual confidence, especially if you can handle them in a light-hearted way. So even brief encounters can be part of the progress towards a more rewarding, long-term partnership.

## 7. Chart Your Journey

Keep a record of your progress if you can. If you have followed the advice in the last chapter you will have already acquired a notebook and will be using it to keep notes on people you contact and meet up with. You could also write a journal about dating; it's a rewarding way of expressing your feelings, and writing can help to tease out the threads from any knotty problems that arise. It's a way of distilling the wisdom from your experience; you may be able to use this to help your own friends in the future.

## 8. Keep Going!

Make the decision to stay strong emotionally. You may be tempted to give up, but remember your aim is to search for love, and so you will keep going whatever the mood of the moment. Don't let momentary disappointments or lacklustre dates sway you from your quest; the saying, 'You have to kiss a lot of frogs before you find a prince' certainly has truth in it. You will almost certainly get there in the end, and perhaps when you're least expecting it.

Keep all your other friendships and activities going, and don't dream too far ahead into a rosy future that hasn't yet materialized.

Dawn gave us this tip for women in the dating arena:

*Invest in your girlfriends, and don't forget about them before, during or after your quest for a man, because they're just too important, and they will always be there whether the men are or not.*

## Keeping Centred

As you begin the process of meeting and engaging with new people, the task of staying centred becomes vital. However accomplished, mature and self-aware each of us may be, we can all be swayed by powerful emotions when entering a new relationship. And it may not be so easy to find an outlet for them in midlife; you may often have to deal with your feelings on your own. Bella, a psychotherapist who fell deeply in love in her early 50s, reflects:

*As you get older, your privacy becomes more important, so the tendency is to keep emotion back and share it only with people who're really close to you. There isn't the same juvenile need to let everybody know about it, to let everybody see, 'Oh, I'm so in love!'*

If you meditate or engage in another spiritual practice, keep it up. It can be tempting to postpone regular practice when things suddenly start happening romantically, but it will help you to stay steady and maintain your sense of identity. You are going through a period of change: whatever happens with dating and relationships, the fact is that you have decided to move your life forward into a new phase. This will inevitably bring new experiences and a certain amount of internal readjustment.

Mundane tasks and routines can also be a blessing, especially if you find yourself on a rollercoaster ride of emotions at some point. Simple activities like digging the garden, washing up and preparing a meal can all be grounding and satisfying. If you find yourself brooding, or perhaps caught in a spiral of excitement, do something practical or go out for a walk in the fresh air.

## Breathing and Body Awareness

These simple but effective exercises can help to re-balance your energy and increase your sense of well being in situations where you feel unsettled or overwhelmed. Practise them ahead of time, before you need them; they are good, basic techniques which can be a useful tool in everyday life too.

### Abdominal Breathing

You're preparing for a date and you can't stop a flutter of nerves threatening to spoil your pleasure in meeting somebody new. Take five minutes and try this breathing exercise, which will help to calm you and is good for your energy levels. You can practise this almost anywhere – standing up, sitting or lying down. Make sure that your legs aren't crossed, that your back is straight and that your body is relaxed.

First of all, focus on your abdomen, sensing it as an important centre of energy in your body. Then breathe out slowly and gently, with lips partially open. Take a comfortable pause, then close your lips and let your tongue rest in the top of your mouth, its tip just touching your upper teeth. Now, keeping your chest still, breathe in through your nose, slowly and deeply, allowing your lower abdomen to expand. Feel the breath flow down into it, filling it like fresh, clear water. When you have reached the full extent of the breath, pause again before releasing the breath out through your lips at the same slow, even tempo. Each out-breath releases stale energy; each in-breath renews your energy. Practise this for a few minutes, in through the nose and out through the mouth, before returning to normal breathing.

Note: Most of the time, our breathing looks after itself. It's very important after breathing exercises to let any conscious control go and return to the natural state, otherwise various forms of tension can build up.

## Body Awareness

Maybe by now you're sitting in a café or restaurant with your date and feeling a little overwhelmed as you try to take in all your impressions. At some point he or she is likely to nip out to the toilet, or head off to settle the bill. Take advantage of this short break and use this technique to bring your attention back into your body, and thus balance your physical and mental state.

Sit comfortably, with a straight back, but stay relaxed. Be still, but alert. Close your eyes if possible, or relax them so that you are gazing down, eyelids half-closed. Let go of any wandering thoughts. Then become aware of your whole body and experience the range of sensations that goes with this. Once you have this going, you can then perform a slow sweep through your body, moving your attention up gradually from your feet to the top of your head. Feel your body as a sensitive, responsive organism which has its own intelligence. It is a source of both information and strength. Then return to your general awareness of your whole body. If you only have a brief interlude before your date returns, just stay with this for a couple of minutes, and remember to switch back to normal mode again afterwards.

When you are at home, or have more time, give it five minutes or so, then get up slowly. Take a few paces around the room. You should feel light, and newly attuned to the world around you afterwards.

## Hopes and Expectations

As well as these active approaches for keeping on course, there are desires and expectations that can affect your progress. These are connected with the key intentions that you formulated earlier, in Chapter 2. There is no such thing as a pure wish to look for love; everything is clothed and coloured to some degree, and we all have ingrained ideas about what love is, and in what form we expect it to come along. However, the important thing is that we don't allow these ideas to remain lurking in the background as outdated versions of our romantic yearnings that can trip us up or impede our search. It's time to bring these ideas out into the open, give them an airing, throw out those that no longer fit and shake the dust off the rest.

## *Keeping an Open Mind*

Angela, a trim woman in her early 60s, had firm views on the men she was prepared to meet. She wanted a well-off man who had risen high in his profession. The dating agency matched her up with several possibilities, but in quick succession she rejected the profiles of a plumber, a local government officer and a travel agent. She wasn't willing to look beyond their job descriptions to the individual who was filling those roles. On top of these expectations, she also required the prospective candidate to have radically green and left-wing political views, and to understand the finer points of wining and dining. She was already well down the route of disappointment, but felt aggrieved with the agency's inability to fulfil her wishes.

None of those expectations was right or wrong in itself, and Angela was in a way being frank about her own views and the kind of person who would match up to those. But the combination she was looking for would be practically impossible to find, especially since personal compatibility and sexual attraction would have to come into play as well.

We've already encouraged you to be realistic about the kind of person you can and can't see yourself with. However, it's also important not to set too many of these requirements in stone, and to know the difference between those that are essential, and those that would be nice but which are by no means 'must haves'. Otherwise, the very formulations that are meant to help you in your search can cut out the light and block the way.

Our advice to Angela would be to meet a wider variety of men to start with, and to see how she finds each one as an individual. Going out on one date with someone doesn't commit you to spending the rest of your life with them. Keep some flexibility in your outlook.

## Soulmates

Many of us would like to find a soulmate. The phrase 'looking for a soulmate' is frequently found on dating sites, and carries a sense of a true and lasting communion with that special person. Rather poignantly, the term 'soulmate' seems to come into its own in midlife; in youth, you are more likely to put your faith into the process of falling in love, and in the passionate attachment that this brings. Older and wiser, you know that being in love is great, but more is needed for a relationship to last, such as genuine companionship and a love that transcends physical looks and the excitement of sex. But although the idea of a soulmate is a beautiful concept, it may be hard to pin down in reality.

For a start, not everyone believes in soulmates, or thinks that they are likely to find one. Martin, with his scientific turn of mind, says: 'My true soulmate might be living in some remote village in China, so I might never meet them.' Some people believe that we can have a number of potential soulmates, whereas others think that there is only one soulmate for each person. Another view, taken by Dawn and Kate, is that soulmates can be close friends of the same sex who seem to share your inner thoughts. So people have different ideas as to what the term means, and expectations could clash if we actively go looking for a soulmate as a partner.

Others are wary of using the term 'soulmate' at all, in the context of real-life relationships: 'I've had deep resonances with people, people I feel a deep level of spiritual connection with, but it never forms itself into the term soulmates,' Adrian reflects. He and Valerie feel that they have a true bond, but not necessarily as soulmates. 'Life experience can change your beliefs,' Cherry's partner, Robert, says. 'You might believe that you've met your soulmate and then the relationship goes under – so what do you believe then?' Perhaps that's why, in our middle years, we are more careful about claiming that someone is our soulmate. We realize that it is largely up to us to forge the relationship, and that whether or not this person is our one true match, the relationship is incredibly precious. Cherishing and keeping that becomes the most important thing. By putting a 'soulmate' label on the relationship, we might actually be endangering it, creating impossibly high expectations that could threaten our confidence when its inevitable imperfections are revealed.

Some people do, however, have genuine experience of finding their soulmate. Thomas, just married for the second time in his 50s, and wary of popular soulmate ideas, says:

*But after all that, I still believe in soulmates! I have experienced the feeling of being one half of the same being, and it's amazingly powerful – one of the very few truly transcendent experiences I've had.*

Bella, too, believes that she and her lover Daniel are soulmates; they are both in their 50s and have been seeing each other for about five years. Bella comes from a medical family with a particularly rational outlook, but on the question of relationships she is passionate:

*I know that I have quite a romantic view. My mother, God bless her, would call it 'a fairy story view'. I believe that there is one special person there. There's a lot who will do, and whom you could have a perfectly happy life with, and be in love with to a certain extent, but there is one particular person whom you are just meant to be with. And he's the one. I have absolutely no doubt about it.*

Whatever your personal beliefs and experiences, try to keep your horizons open. Even if you hope to find a soulmate, we recommend that you look beyond that hope, towards a partner whom you could love and share your life with in a meaningful way, even if he or she is not 'the one' in that way. Love can come in different guises, and by being prepared to go beyond your usual expectations you may find a truer kind of love than you have ever done before.

## Looking into the Future

The future holds a strong fascination for most people, and many of us have a sense that we can have access to knowledge about it, perhaps through our own intuition or dreams, or else through a 'reading'. A large number of people consult psychics or have their horoscopes interpreted or Tarot cards read. Not everything in such readings is predictive; much is related to our character and potential. They can be enlightening, and also reassuring in times of crisis and stress. However, they can also create too high a level of expectation as we become involved in proactive dating. Any prediction involving the future has to be taken with caution. We cannot be absolutely certain of what will happen in our lives, and all these readings and revelations come through human, fallible channels. Sometimes the most astonishing alignment of predictions may occur, which still don't come true, as Sue, a divorced woman in her mid-50s discovered. She was eager to start a new relationship, and for a while tried to find some clues to the future from clairvoyant readings:

*I have consulted quite a few psychics over the years, sometimes close together, but the predictions haven't always had a lot in common. But there was one year when four different psychics said I was going to meet a man before the end of February. I spent the next few months actively going out to places where I might meet guys, but in the end I never did.*

Having a reading can be helpful, but we suggest that you keep any references to the future in mind as interesting information, not cast-iron facts. By all means use tips and leads you are given, but treat them in the same way as you would any other advice given, including the guidelines in this book: as useful pointers, navigation tools which you can try out along the way. Otherwise it is possible to become enslaved to even the finest words of wisdom. We are ultimately responsible for making our own choices, and this is where freedom lies, and often the best outcome too.

## Twists and Turns of Fate

It's often said that there is some quirk of fate operating when true partners meet for the first time. You miss the train – and your future husband just happens to be sitting opposite you on the next one that you catch. You decide to go in one direction, but something beyond your control seems to propel you in another, and there you find love in an unexpected way. Stephanie booked up at the last minute for the walking holiday where she met Martin, and Cherry met Robert on a cruise after accepting an invitation to lecture very late in the day. While on board, the sad news came through that Robert's father had died, which rapidly deepened the bond between them, in a way that might not have happened otherwise in the short two weeks at sea.

This may seem to rule out proactive dating as a way to find your match, with its carefully selected profiles and deliberately arranged meetings. However, Kate believes that fate may have lent a helping hand in bringing her and Douglas together through the introduction agency:

*I feel very lucky that Doug and I met the way we did. We certainly wouldn't have met otherwise – we lived a long way from each other. I can't see how our paths would have crossed. And because we're very different, maybe if we'd met at a party or something we wouldn't have talked to each other! Perhaps this is the only way we would have found each other.*

Chance meetings and unexpected events often play a crucial part in making a new bond. Yet we can't rely on these, and can't manufacture them. And this is not an argument for giving up a proactive search, because the search creates not only the framework for so-called fate to operate in, but also a magnetic power that helps to draw two people closer together. It comes back to the old saying that we mentioned right at the start: 'God will provide, but you must lay your own knife and fork.'

Further on we give some examples of how coincidences, dreams and events in the world around us can be extraordinarily powerful and accurate significators in meeting someone, and in casting light on a new relationship. We encourage you to be aware of these, but at the same time to keep your own powers of discrimination active. You have set up this search, and your volition is crucial in activating the process. Even when it seems as if the universe is taking over and managing the flow of circumstances in a way that you could not have dreamed of, who is to say whether that was something destined to come your way anyway, or whether you have helped to trigger this by your efforts? Keep both your own intention going and your personal faith in the meaning of events, and the chances are high that you will find what, or whom, you are looking for.

In this chapter we have set up the road map for the journey that you're taking, and given you some signposts to help you on your way. We've encouraged you to keep an open mind, so that you can vary the route if need be, but still stay focused on your destination. If you can remain both outwardly observant and inwardly reflective as you begin to gather information about other people by email or phone, you'll find that these are invaluable skills on a first date, when you'll be able to glean and interpret crucial details about the person you're meeting in a very short space of time. It's these vital phone calls and intriguing first dates that we'll move on to now.

CHAPTER SEVEN

# *Getting Acquainted*

As soon as you're ready to start dating, you'll be in direct contact with other individuals who are also looking for love: you'll be connecting on the phone and on dates and, hopefully, taking the first steps towards forging a new relationship before too long. Careful preparation and setting up your strategy have got you to this point, and will surely support you in this exciting new phase. But going live requires keeping that all-important balance of a cool head and a warm heart, and the further practical guidelines that we give here can help you to do just that.

## Phone Calls

Before you meet someone for a first date, you're likely to speak to them on the phone. On the face of it, a phone call is a simple thing, but it carries a lot of weight in the early stages of proactive dating, and often determines whether the two of you decide to meet up or not. You may be quite at ease chatting to a stranger on the phone; Kate was used to doing this for her work, and wasn't daunted: 'By talking to people I can usually tell whether there is enough in common, enough interests to make me want to meet them. It's a good filter.' Or you could find it something of an ordeal, like Martin: 'The whole business of contacting people you know nothing about, never spoken to before, I found difficult. It seemed quite strained, an unnatural situation.'

But with the right approach and armed with a few leading questions, you will be more confident about speaking to a potential date, and can discover most of what you need to know at this point. Here are some suggestions as to how to go about it.

## Be Polite, But Ask the Right Questions

- Be considerate. If you are the one making the phone call, ask if it's convenient to talk now, and keep the call to a reasonable length of time, perhaps to a maximum of 20 minutes.

- Ask about their age, their work and interests, where they live and what their relationship status is. Even if you already have some of the information, it's helpful to hear how they talk about it. If they are divorced, separated or a widower/widow, try to find out how long they have been on their own.

- Be ready to give out the same essential facts about yourself, and to fill in your background a little more, but you don't have to give them your life history at this stage.

- If you can, find out what kind of a relationship they are looking for in a general sense (long-term, friendship, casual, etc.).

- Don't ask very personal or intrusive questions, for instance about their finances or their weight.

- Safeguard your privacy. Withhold your number before calling, if it's from a landline, and don't give out your landline number during the conversation unless you want to and are confident that the person is 100 per cent genuine.

- Note your responses. If the person annoys or upsets you, even in some trivial way, it can mean that your personalities may be at odds with one another, something that can show up right from the start.

- Don't expect sexual chemistry on the phone. Wait until the first or second date to see whether there is a spark. Watch out for overtly sexy chat from the other person, however, as this is a sign that they are looking for fun rather than a committed relationship.

- Finish the call when you have had enough. 'It's been lovely talking to you, but I have one or two other calls to make' should do the trick.

All these indicators will help you to decide whether you might like to meet up with this person. If handling a phone call seems tricky or stilted at first, keep going! As you begin to have more of these conversations you will become acclimatized to them, and they'll become easier. You'll also find that even a short chat, carefully handled, gives you a great deal of information, both verbal and emotional. As you learn to decode this you will begin to recognize more readily whether the person is a possible match for you or not. It's often a question of weighing up your impressions overall, which gets easier with practice.

Remember that making or taking a phone call does not commit you to a date with that person. You're simply having a chat to find out more about each other, and you needn't agree to meet unless you already know for sure that you want to do so. If the other person tries to press you for an answer, be polite but firm: 'It's been nice talking to you, and I'd like to think about it. Can I call you back if it looks possible?' Make sure you have their number before you hang up. If you handle it this way, remember that the ball will be in your court. Don't expect to be chased. People in this situation are sensitive to signs of possible rejection, so if you really do fancy meeting up once you've thought about it, ring back and say so.

## Going Forward

You may find that you have two or three phone calls with someone before you arrange to see them for the first time. Perhaps you live some distance apart, or maybe busy times at work mean that a date has to be put on hold for a little while. But in general, you'll want to meet without too much delay. It's not worth extending phone chats indefinitely, or collecting lame dogs along the way. If they procrastinate about meeting you, they may be juggling with a lot of other possible candidates, or reluctant to turn phone rapport into reality. Philip, a gardener, responded eagerly to an ad and rang up several times for a cozy chat. When the woman concerned finally put the question, 'Well, would you like to meet up?' he backed off in a hurry. 'Oh, I'm not sure. It's so nice, talking like this. Meeting could spoil it, couldn't it?'

Here are two specific and important areas to consider as you talk to someone, either on the phone or on a first date. They are questions for which it is hard to give fixed answers, so you will have to interpret each situation as it arises. Both instances are areas which come up fairly frequently, and in which other people frequently try to overstep the boundaries, so think about these issues in advance, and decide whether you'll be willing to make exceptions or not.

## *Relationship Status*

Would you consider a person who is separated, rather than divorced or widowed? Among our interviewees, opinions were divided: Martin was quite clear in his mind that he would never entertain such a possibility, whereas Kate was prepared to be with Douglas before his divorce came through. If you wouldn't rule out seeing a separated person, then during a phone chat or first date try to get a clear idea of what stage they are at. Dig a little deeper, if necessary. It does happen that people begin to date before they are clearly separated, and you may find that certain individuals advertising themselves as separated are still living under the same roof as their partner, or even, as one woman ruefully put it, 'separated but the wife doesn't know about it'. The first is a minefield, the second is pure deception, and both offer affairs rather than relationships.

On the other hand, there are many people who are genuinely separated, often with legal agreements to this effect, or who have been living completely independent lives for a long time. But it can be tricky working out whether they are really looking for a new partner, or if they are still tied into their marriage in some way.

*Cherry: Randal was very open about the fact that he was separated when we spoke on the phone, and I thought this was fine because he and his wife had been apart for years. She was ill, and lived permanently in a nursing home. He had brought up two daughters almost single-handed, which was admirable. However, as I got to know him better I realized that there was a whole tangle of dependency which hadn't been sorted out. He was frightened to divorce in case the in-laws thought badly of him, had failed to commit to a passionate love affair because of this in the recent past, and was still totally entwined with his grown-up, 20-something daughters. When Randal and I had dinner together for the first time, one of them rang up three times during the meal for advice and support, which he gave her at length. Looking back, I realize that I brushed aside these signs and other misgivings right at the start, when I should have taken notice of them.*

Lara had a similar experience with James, with whom she was seriously involved for 18 months:

*Lara: Despite what he had told me when we first met, I realized that he wasn't going to fully leave his marriage in the foreseeable future. His wife was living with another man, and had been for many years, which was why I believed James when he told me that the fact that they hadn't yet divorced wasn't a barrier to our relationship. But over time it became clear that they hadn't divorced because they were both reluctant to finally sever the marriage. He spent almost every holiday with his wife, her partner and the grown-up children, and there was no space for him to form a real partnership with a new person.*

So beware! Failure to move on can be a real affliction in midlife, and the sense of responsibility to children and ex-partners can in some cases make it impossible to start again. If you meet someone in this situation, check out the whole scene before you become emotionally attached.

Whatever you decide in terms of a person's marital position, bear in mind that ultimately divorce does make a difference, and although you may strike up a wonderful and lasting relationship with someone who is separated, there is still often a difficult stage that the separated person needs to go through in order to be completely free to enter a new relationship fully. You may have to take a gamble that they will do this.

## Age

This is one of the most fraught areas of dating. Women complain that men expect to take up with someone 25 years younger than themselves; men complain that women lie about their age. Lack of confidence in oneself can be one of the reasons for this, or a desperate drive to try and prove that you are not as old as the numbers say. We all want to be living proof that we are in the vigorous prime of life, and some Internet daters boast of putting their 'real' age online (the age they feel inside), rather than their 'chronological' one (as measured by their birth certificate). But we have clocked up those years, and they do show.

We don't recommend lying about your age; in any serious relationship the truth will soon come to light, and then there will be issues of deception to deal with. A small 'white' lie in this context can set the wrong tone for the relationship, and undermines the beginnings of trust that two people want to build up with each other. It's also advisable in general to keep to the age limits that other people specify in their criteria for a partner. Respect their boundaries, just as you want other people to respect yours.

Have confidence that your age is not a problem! Yes, it's true that the social climate may favour the young, and that as you get older you may have fewer responses to an ad. But love really can come at any age, and you don't need 50 replies to sift through, flattering though that may be. You are individual and unique, and there is someone out there ready to respond to that, who will love you for who you are. And in the meantime, it's not an all-or-nothing situation. Most of our interviewees in their 40s had plenty of responses to choose from, those in their 50s and 60s perhaps somewhat fewer, but still enough for interesting dates and interim relationships before they came across their future partners.

When you decide on the upper and lower age limit of people that you want to meet, be realistic but review it every so often, in case it is too lenient or restricted. Don't be tempted to abandon your criteria entirely, though. It's tempting to think that 'the right person' could be any age at all, but the chances are that he or she will in fact be similar in years to you. Anthony, beginning to date again at 68, dreamed that he might find a Russian woman doctor in her 40s, but in reality was happy to meet women in the 55+ age bracket, and thrilled to meet Claudia, then aged around 60, as his match.

Claudia herself met a number of men via newspaper ads, and not all were what they seemed in terms of age:

*The most priceless one sounded promising on the phone, as he had a great sense of humour and we had plenty in common. 'I'm just a teensy bit over your age range,' he said. (I had specified a maximum age of*

65.) *As I sat waiting in the pub car park I saw a very elderly looking gentleman arrive in an open-topped sports car. My immediate instinct was to think, 'How quickly can I get out of this without appearing to be rude?' After a hasty sandwich lunch I announced that I had to go, and he asked when we would meet again. 'We won't be doing that,' I said. 'Why not?' he asked. 'Well,' I said, 'I think you've been telling me porkie pies. Come on, 'fess up.' He then admitted to being 80! He said he didn't want to meet women of his own age because they were all so old.*

Cherry, in her mid-50s, had a number of calls from men in their late 60s and 70s, even though she had said clearly that she wanted to meet someone no more than five years older than herself:

*It was always a giveaway if they didn't mention their age when they left a message for me. And if I did call back, a lot of hedging went on before I could coax the truth out of them! They would often ask me why I minded, which was embarrassing. 'But I don't feel my age!' they protested. I wanted to say that it was to do with life expectancy, but rather than be blunt I sometimes said, 'Well, it works the other way round too. I wouldn't want to have a relationship with someone 15 or 20 years younger than myself, because the age gap would be too great.' That usually left them bemused, and gave me time to slide out of the conversation gracefully!*

## The First Date
### Valerie and Adrian's First Date
As you may recall from Chapter 4, Adrian had to convince Valerie that it would be a good idea to meet up. Although they had been emailing each other for several weeks, Valerie was wary, but she did finally agree to see him when he next came up to Birmingham.

*Adrian:* Even the process of getting to that was interesting. I said, 'What shall we do? I'll come and pick you up at your house.' But I could feel her backing off again. So I said, 'Let's not talk about it now. Whatever you're comfortable with, I'll go along with. You just decide what you want to do.' I passed all the control to her.

*Valerie:* Yes, and that worked. I think if you'd insisted on coming to the house, then the date wouldn't have happened.

After careful reflection, she suggested that they should meet in the Buddhist room of the city museum because of their common interest in Buddhism. (As we saw in Chapter 1, Adrian had been a Buddhist monk for many years before leaving his order for secular life.)

*Valerie:* You do want to be safe, and in a public place when you meet for the first time. And also to be able to walk away without it being too embarrassing or difficult if you realize it's a big mistake. I was so nervous. I had to come from work, and I was walking up towards the art gallery thinking, 'I don't have to do this, I could just walk away.' He was actually waiting on the balcony and watched me walk through, so he was keeping his options open too.

*Adrian:* I was like a cat on hot bricks. She had mentioned that she liked Green and Black's chocolate so I'd gone to Sainsbury's and bought every kind that they had. And I was thinking that I could do something crazy, like dropping the chocolate at her feet from the balcony. But, of course, the odds on that going horribly wrong were rather high! So I came down the stairs when I saw her coming, and it was kind of reassuring for both of us that we were each nervous and a bit fumbling.

*And then you think, 'Should we hug or shake hands?' We did none of that, and just looked at each other. When you meet someone normally you don't have all those cards on the table, that you want a relationship, and so you bring those things out very tentatively as you feel into the territory. But what's so good in this situation is that you get through that immediately, because there's a clarity about why you are both there. We went for tea and cake, and then walked around the exhibition, and it just felt very comfortable.*

After the museum, they took a stroll.

*Adrian: I hadn't walked around the centre of Birmingham for years. This was nice, because it was a place we both knew from our childhoods.*

Then, as they were still comfortable in each other's company, and wanted more time together, they went to another cafe.

*Valerie: I drank your coffee because I didn't like mine!*

*Adrian: Yes, I gave you my coffee.*

*Valerie: I was quite impressed by that.*

*Adrian: Then I offered to drive you home.*

Valerie, who had decided in advance that she wouldn't accept a lift on a first date, told him, much to her own surprise: 'You seem to be having quite an effect on me, so I'm going to say yes.'

*Valerie: We started holding hands then.*

*Adrian: There was a strong charge between us. In these situations previously I would most often have felt that I didn't want to open any further, as a kind of warning sign. With Valerie I didn't feel any of that. There was just a feeling of relaxation.*

He drove Valerie home, and when they got there her sons were in. This was where Valerie was ready to finish the date.

**Valerie:** *I hadn't told them what I was up to, so I didn't invite you in.*

**Adrian:** *We just sat in the car for a while and I asked if you were free on the Sunday and you said yes. We had a slight embrace, a little hug. But even those little things were very powerful, and had a big impact. I just stroked your head very slightly and –*

**Valerie:** *I was a goner!*

**Adrian:** *It just flowed – there was no forcing from my side, and I could read the signs easily. It wasn't awkward between us. It was clear to me when to pull back, and I did.*

This wonderful account of a first date is not only a touching story, but also brings out many of the elements that can be crucial to the success of a meeting. Normally, first dates are only for an hour or so, something we'll come to shortly, but this continued for much longer because the two of them proved to be so compatible, and thoughtful about the way they handled its progress. Following their story through, we can see how sensitively they responded to each other, which enabled them to go beyond the usual limits. Guidelines for a first date are there for our self-protection, but when we meet someone exceptional we may decide to break the rules, just as they did.

Even before Adrian and Valerie met, they had to prepare carefully and keep the rapport going. Their frequent exchange of emails had helped to open the channels of communication, but when it came to a real, live meeting, it wasn't so easy. They were both full of anticipation, and Valerie was very nervous. Adrian kept up the impetus when she began to waver, but wisely stepped back at the critical moment, inviting Valerie to take control.

This put her more at ease, and she was able to think through the best way to meet. Sensibly, she suggested meeting at an easy time of day and in a public place. There was no agenda to have a meal or spend a fixed amount of time together, which could have created too much pressure. Both of them brought a beautiful personal touch to the date – Valerie by choosing the Buddhist room, and Adrian by buying her favourite chocolate.

They were able to decide in a relaxed way to extend the meeting, by strolling through the streets where they had both spent their childhoods (establishing common ground is a good thing to do on a first date) and then going for another coffee. Their approach to each other went at an easy pace: eye contact, followed by a sedate taking of the arm as they walked together, then holding hands, and finally a gentle hug. Just before they parted, physical attraction blazed up, but that became a promise for their future contact, not something to act on in the moment.

Adrian and Valerie's story shows one way in which a date can work out for the best. It's a living example of how two people delicately handled the dynamics of a first meeting and brought the best out of their initial contact. But, like all real-life stories, it is unique; as well as the encouragement their success gives us, we need to think about the more general guidelines that we might want to use on a first date too.

## What to Do on a First Date

*Safety*

The obvious rule of safety is to meet in a public place. Although the chances of meeting a maniac on a date are slim, nevertheless there is no point in taking chances. If you are a woman, you might also want to tell a friend where you're going, and arrange to call them by a certain time to say you're safely home again. Take a mobile phone with you if possible. Don't accept a lift to the meeting place, or back home again unless, like Valerie, all your doubts have been dispelled. A daytime rendezvous is good, but not always possible; early evening dates can be useful as you can always plead a later engagement, if necessary.

## How, When and Where

The aim of the first date is to meet someone face to face, to get to know a little more about them and to help you both decide whether you want to take it further.

Meeting up simply for a cup of coffee or tea is often the best solution to the awkward question of what to do. Meeting for a drink is also a popular option, but beware of one drink leading to another, and another, and then … By the way, if you don't want to drink alcohol, it's perfectly possible to meet in a pub or wine bar and have a soft drink. You may find that your date does exactly the same, especially if he or she is driving.

It's a nice gesture for the man to invite the woman to choose where to meet, as Adrian did with Valerie. When deciding on the place, avoid cafés or bars that are too noisy, otherwise you'll be shouting at each other for the duration. Hotels can be excellent, as you can often order tea or drinks while relaxing in easy chairs in the lounge, and country pubs or riverside inns may also be spacious, pleasant places to meet, with opportunities for sitting outside if the weather's fine. Galleries and exhibitions, as Valerie discovered, can sometimes make a good first date if you're both interested in what's on display, though keep it to a manageable selection rather than a marathon sight-seeing tour, and be prepared for the fact that you may find your real point of focus is the tea room. Much will be determined by your location and the venues on offer. It's a good idea to keep a short list of possible meeting places in mind, or ready to hand in your notebook, when you're handling phone calls and emails, otherwise your mind may suddenly go blank if you're asked for a suggestion.

We strongly recommend that the first date is kept short. Planning to meet for an hour to an hour and a half is just about right, though some people do inevitably want to spend longer if it goes really well, as Valerie and Adrian did, and as Kate and Douglas also found on their first meeting. 'We arranged to meet for lunch in Oxford. I was surprised how well we got on!' said Kate. 'So we decided to go for a long walk, and then to have tea.'

If you do decide in advance to go for a meal, bear in mind that it commits you for a couple of hours, and can be awkward if things don't go smoothly.

*Cherry: Every time I broke my own rule of just going out for tea or coffee, I regretted it. I love eating out, so it was a bit of a temptation for me. But for one thing, it extended the contact far too long. Even with people I liked, I found myself tired after an hour or so. It's an intense business, getting to know someone else at close quarters, talking all the time. And with those I didn't like, I couldn't wait to get away.*

*Most dates were very pleasant, but I had a couple that weren't. There was one guy who talked non-stop about steam trains. And another who sounded nearly perfect – he was good-looking, cultured, and we had many overlapping interests. Full of optimism, we arranged to meet at a rather nice Italian restaurant. But the moment we met, we took an instant dislike to one another! I found him too smooth and arrogant and I don't think that he was very taken with me, either. I couldn't wait to get away, but we had to sit politely through the meal first, which was very difficult.*

Beware, too, of giving in to pressure to spend extra time on the date because the person is driving a long distance to see you, or wants to make a day of it. You're not under any obligation to do this; Adrian and Valerie, and Kate and Douglas, generously gave each other more time because they genuinely wanted to, not because they thought they ought to. It's best to make it clear in advance that the plan is to meet up for an hour and, if necessary, to plead other appointments or commitments on that day. If someone really wants to meet you, they'll accept these terms.

## First Date Guidelines

Here are a few extra suggestions for helping the first date to go smoothly.

- If you haven't already seen the person's photo on a website, exchange photographs before you meet, if possible. If not, then give each other a clear idea of what you look like, and whereabouts you'll aim to be sitting or standing.

- Be punctual. Your date will appreciate it, and remember that in practical terms, car-parking limits or later appointments could shorten the time you can spend together if one of you is late.

- Be warm and polite. Even if you can see that the other person isn't your type, this is still a chance to get to know someone new. Being friendly will help you to enjoy the date too, and leave you with positive memories, even if it never goes any further.

- Be ready to share the bill. This is usually considered fair practice on a first date, though if the man wants to pay the woman can graciously give way if she chooses. Or not, if she wants to avoid any sense of obligation. Meeting for a coffee or a drink makes this less of an issue, as the expenses are small.

## Body Language

Reams have been written in the last few decades about body language, which is now the focus of specialist studies and training practices. It's said that body language conveys far more information than speech, so it's certainly worth paying attention to how people sit, look and move on a date. However, unless you are expert in the subject, a gentle, general awareness is all that's needed here. You don't need to be too self-conscious about it, or feel that you have to try too hard. And above all, be authentic; don't try to manipulate the other person through body language.

Here are a few basic points, which will help to dissolve any nervousness or shyness that you feel, and should also help both of you to relax. Be ready to put them into practice, but also take notice of what your body tells you; when we can't meet someone's gaze, or sit at ease with them, it often indicates an instinctive wariness on our part which may indicate a general lack of compatibility between the two people, or perhaps an element of pretence on the other person's part.

- Make eye contact when you first meet, and frequently afterwards. Long, languorous stares are not needed, but friendly looks are good.

- Shake hands. This might seem a little formal, but it gives the chance to have some harmless physical contact with the other person, and to decide whether you like the sense of their energy and touch.

- Choose seating positions which are comfortable, if you can. If you are in an informal venue, such as a hotel lounge, you may prefer to sit at an angle to each other. Some people find this more relaxed and less intense for a first date. Others prefer to sit opposite one another, face to face, which gives the opportunity for plenty of eye contact and to observe the other person directly.

- Try to take up 'open' positions, with arms relaxed, hands loose or upturned, and chest open. By the same token, avoid 'closed' positions, with arms crossed or fists clenched, which are a sign of keeping to yourself and warding off other people. Even if shyness is the cause, they will have an adverse effect on the person you're meeting.

- Take a moment to breathe a little slower and deeper every now and then. This will help to centre you and to give you confidence. Keep the breath light, or it could look a little odd.

- See if the two of you do any mirroring, by adopting the same position or gesture. This is usually a gesture of empathy, performed unconsciously, and shows that you feel in tune with one another. Mirroring is a subtle thing, however, and a little goes a long way. Too much mirroring from one person can indicate that they are trying too hard to please – if it's you, sit back now and then. It can also be a learned technique, designed to get someone on your side, as in salesmanship, for instance, so be a little careful if the other person seems to mirror you deliberately.

## Handling the Conversation
*Slow-release Information*

Your first face-to-face chat with someone has the practical aim of finding out a little more about each other, to go somewhat further with the facts that you've already gleaned through emails or phone calls. This requires co-operation from both people, so don't play at being mysterious or hard to get, in terms of the conversation. You've already signed up to the encounter, which carries with it an implicit understanding that you'll be communicative. Be willing to give out the key facts about yourself, and let your personality come through. The art of the first-date conversation is to handle it in as natural a way as possible. It's a chat between potential friends rather than a job interview, so pick your moments to ask the more serious questions, such as the type of relationship the other person might be looking for.

Although it's great to be friendly, do hold something back. 'As my old Scottish granny always used to say, keep your powder dry!' advises one friend of Cherry's. Kate too suggests caution: 'You don't want to divulge too much about yourself, and don't open your heart and soul unless you know you can take it further. You need to keep some sort of a guard up.' It's amazing how much people in this situation will sometimes reveal about their past lovers, their childhood hang-ups or money battles with the ex. Keep your own output to measured doses, your personal details on slow release. You don't really know the person you're sitting with yet, and can't assume that he or she will be your lifelong partner and confidant. Even if you like each other very much on first sight, you are not yet fully connected, and too much confession can lead to a sense that the person spilling it all out is needy, or bitter, or insecure. You may also need to curb anyone (in a kindly way, if possible) who rattles on and on. You signed up for a date, not to be a counsellor or a passive listener.

## Keeping the Balance

The aim is to keep the date enjoyable, not to endure it as an ordeal. So in talking, try to find a dynamic that you're both comfortable with, and which will keep the energy balanced between you.

It's important that each of you listens to the other, and each of you is interested in the other, if the relationship is to have a chance. Two people may have different degrees of talkativeness, but there should be a readiness from both sides to talk and to listen, to ask and respond to questions. Anyone who can't do that may have a poor record of relating, so take note right now if you are going to set much store by communication in the future.

## Pace and Progress

Anthony was keen to make quick progress when he first met Claudia, but had to restrain himself as he was in danger of scaring her off. Now happily married, they compared their experience of that first date:

*Anthony: I suppose I could have blown it on the first meeting when I said 'You're the one – let's get together!'*

*Claudia: You nearly did – you frightened me!*

*Anthony (horrified): Could I have lost you?*

*Claudia: I went and collected some coffee for us – I thought the situation needed defusing. You certainly did startle me. That was pretty full-on.*

*Anthony: Well, that was the point of our meeting.*

*Claudia: No. The point was to see if we liked each other. And it takes time to establish trust.*

In Anthony's eyes, his approach was perfectly reasonable; he and Claudia had met up to figure out if they might make good partners, so why not tell her so? After all, she might slip through the net otherwise. But Claudia was wary of disappointments, from past encounters with men who said what they didn't mean, and it would have been naïve of her to say yes immediately.

The dating arena is a hothouse, an exceptional situation where you are making intense use of short periods of contact to learn what you can about the other person. But don't allow any sense of urgency to predominate; the two people meeting do need to manage the pace gently, and to make allowances for each other. Despite the unusual context it still pays to take it easy, to perform the dance of courtship and response just as you would in everyday life.

## How's It Going?
### *It's the Little Things that Count*

First dates are a great way of learning about other people, in all sorts of little ways. We can discover a lot about someone's character by the things that they do and say. Cherry met one man, a wealthy finance manager, who complained about the price of a pot of tea in the hotel where they were meeting, and another who walked two miles to the date rather than pay for parking. Lara went for tea with a man who insisted she pay for both of them as he had had to pay for parking. We both felt that this kind of behaviour suggested a tightness and lack of generosity that were at odds with the characteristics we would appreciate in a man.

Valerie noted that Adrian gave her his cup of coffee when hers didn't taste right, and Douglas spotted Kate wiping a little bit of gravy off her plate with her finger, which he thought was rather endearing! Small acts of kindness can mean a great deal, and even lapses of conventional manners can suggest feeling at ease in someone's company.

Finding that you act naturally around someone is a good sign; feeling comfortable is an indication that you can be yourself with that person. It doesn't always signify a budding relationship, but it can suggest a growing understanding between you. And if you're lucky, a sense of closeness can develop surprisingly quickly. Stephanie said, of the holiday where she met Martin, 'What was really interesting was that we acted like a couple from the beginning, before we even got together. We sat together at mealtimes all the time.'

## Taking the Temperature between You

Some people know quickly whether there is a spark between them. Anthony was confident of judging the potential chemistry, and scribbled on one profile from the introduction agency, 'Don't fancy her bed-wise,' without asking for a date.

*I got it right with Claudia, and I know why. You've got to be sure when finding a new partner that the chemistry is right. It's the feeling that you want to be close to that person. You feel physically attracted, and not necessarily sex-wise, but that is part of it – a nice little bonus, shall we say?*

Stephanie, too, was always clear at the end of a first date whether there was any potential: 'At our age, you know when you're attracted to a guy or not, and whether they are to you. You're much better at reading the messages.'

This fast response isn't true for everyone, though. Bella was contacted by Daniel, whom she had known slightly in her schooldays, through the Friends Reunited website. They decided to meet up, and started a friendship which continued for several months before the sexual attraction kicked in and they became lovers.

Don't expect flames of desire to blaze up during a first date. Introduction agencies often advise waiting until a second meeting at least before deciding if you are attracted to someone or not. Nerves, expectation and preconceptions about the other person can often colour your initial response. And it helps to know your own pattern, and whether you usually need time to warm up. Go easy on yourself, and if you like the other person enough to see them again, give the physical attraction time to develop. And yes, we all know of cases where first dates intended as polite chats over coffee have ended up in bed, but it isn't usually such a great idea, not if you want the relationship to develop further.

We suggest that you simply enjoy any sexual spark that's kindled without acting on it too quickly. Otherwise you might regret it later, and it can also cause the other person to back off sharply – sometimes a full-on, intimate encounter is too much to handle straight away, especially if they are still in emotional recovery.

## Ending the Date

The date is drawing to a close and it's time to say your goodbyes. How should you end it? Do you decide on the spot whether to meet again? Ideally, it's a good idea to see how you feel after a day or two. You may be over-optimistic simply because you have survived the date well, or are too polite to refuse a follow-up date. Allowing some time for post-date reflection should give you a better chance to check out your underlying responses. A short gap before renewing contact is unlikely to undermine any real pull between you.

If the other person presses you for an answer, you can suggest that the best way forward is usually to think it over for a few days, and then to get in touch with each other. This makes it less of a personal rebuff, and also indicates that you may be seeing other people. It's surprising, but not everyone takes this into account, and someone you meet on a date may assume that he or she is the only potential fish in the sea.

However you decide to handle it, try to avoid giving mixed messages, or making offers that you won't follow up. 'We've both got each other's numbers' is a typical smokescreen, which usually decodes as, 'It's been nice meeting you, but I don't think we'll be seeing each other again.' And experience shows that eager promises to call you very soon don't always materialize. Most people mean well, but can get carried away by the pleased feelings they have when a date has gone well, and may find on second thoughts that they don't want to take it any further. It helps to stay philosophical about this, and to understand that other people are also vulnerable to changeable emotions. Not everyone thinks through the consequences of starting a new relationship before they go on a date. The best you can do is to work out your own game plan, be considerate to those you're meeting, and end with a pleasant farewell rather than a promise that you can't fulfil.

Be wary still of giving your landline number, or your postal address, unless you are really confident about the other person's character. Ian, an ex-chief of police, found that even with his training he wasn't quite careful enough about personal security, and was plagued with phone calls from a schoolteacher he had met on a date, who would ring him in a state of drunken misery every time she felt lonely. It's useful to exchange email addresses, so that if you need to let someone down gently you can do so without making an embarrassing phone call. In general, don't text to refuse another meeting; for the 40+ age group this can come across as insulting.

So when you say goodbye, how do you actually handle it physically? It depends on how much you liked each other, of course, on the first meeting, but a friendly handshake is usually fine as the minimum – after all, you've each made an effort to be there, so you can acknowledge this even if you weren't attracted.

It might seem strange to be touching on the finer points of etiquette like this, but it's the little things that can puzzle us as we start out on the dating path again. A kiss on the cheeks or lips, or a brief hug is a common way of parting, too. The other person's touch may convey how warmly they feel about you, and it can be nice to sense such a connection, whether you meet again or not. Even one-off dates can end affectionately, and this is a good morale booster.

If you've successfully navigated your way through the first date, if you like each other and agree to meet again, you're ready to head into the next stage. And when two people begin to focus on each other, finding out all about the other person and the emotional experience of the connection become the key elements in this new phase. From now on, although we will still give you practical suggestions, it will be the psychological aspects of finding a new partner that take first place in the guidance that we offer.

# CHAPTER EIGHT

# Following Through

So, you've met someone you like, and they like you. You've exchanged emails and phone calls, and had a first date. Now it's time to meet up again. What do you need to stay aware of while enjoying the first shimmering of romance? How do you step through the opening gates into a new relationship without your mutual baggage getting in the way and tripping you up? What do your thoughts, dreams and feelings tell you about this potential new love? How can you make the most of this special time and still stay grounded?

## The Early Stage of Romance

This is a very exciting stage, and if you've met the right someone it can light you up inside. The beginning few dates set the mould for the relationship, and the more romantic the settings you choose, the better. This phase can also be nerve-wracking, depending on your temperament, your past experience and your stage in life. Relax! Enjoy it! You haven't made a commitment yet: you're just exploring new territory together.

The first few dates offer you a ton of information about each other and about how you function together, before there is a pattern laid down. This gives you the chance to feel out the relationship from a truly open perspective.

If the first few dates are positive and special, the memory of this period can keep you in the relationship for long enough to work through any difficulties which emerge after your mutual best behaviour wears off.

The early stages of any enterprise tell us a great deal about how it will continue, so it is worth paying attention to what happens and how you feel, and making notes after each encounter.

## Types of Dates and What They Reveal

Activity dates such as walking, cycling or playing tennis help you see how your energy works together. How does it feel to walk alongside each other? Is your energy compatible? Does it feel good to move alongside this person? Are you having fun?

Cultural dates, like going to an art exhibition or a movie, give you something in the present moment to talk about that is relatively impersonal. This can free things up, especially if one or both of you are feeling nervous. Doing something cultural together, however lowbrow or highbrow, gives you an idea about each other's sensibilities and ways of thinking and feeling about the world. It's a way of exploring mutual interests and your intellectual and cultural compatibility.

Dates over long dinners give you the opportunity to look into each other's eyes and connect at the soul level, to see how you feel in this person's presence. Do you feel warmed? Do you feel seen? Is there a real connection here? Are you sincerely interested in this person?

## Finding Out about Each Other

It's usually best to keep your first few dates to just the two of you. Involving friends and family members too soon can get in the way of figuring out how you get along together as a burgeoning couple. Other people's influence, whether spoken or simply felt, can be confusing. It can make one or both of you feel rushed into a commitment before you are ready, or it can create an atmosphere in which other people's needs take precedence over the process of getting to know each other.

The first few dates are good times to ask bold and leading questions as long as you don't overdo it. You haven't committed to each other in any way, so as long as you are sensitive, questions will be most likely taken at face value. Once you have become more intimate, and established that you are indeed having a relationship, it can become more difficult to ask probing questions until later on, when a deep trust has been created. Once engaged in the relationship you may be less inclined to want unwelcome answers, and questions may be interpreted as neurotic or distrusting when you already know each other a bit, but not enough to trust each other completely. This of course depends on the individual relationship. Hopefully you will be building an atmosphere of clear and open communication, but there are always sensitive moments in the timing of intimacy, and it's as well not to miss the opportunity that the first few dates offer, as long as you don't give your date a grilling and put them off by being too intrusive.

You have a certain amount of information already from your initial emails and phone calls, but there are some questions you need to ask face to face. If the person does have anything to hide or gloss over, it is easier to fob you off with a partial answer through email or over the phone. Conversely, if you need reassurance about anything, this will be more convincing if you are physically present with each other. This can be particularly important in the territory of the newly separated, to see whether they really are free or not.

The first date is usually too short to get into a lot of detail, and is mainly to see if there is enough of an attraction to warrant meeting up again. The second, third and fourth dates reveal a great deal of information: so much so that it can be hard to keep it all clear in your mind, and keeping a journal will help you, especially if you are dating several people at once in the early stages.

A large part of getting to know someone comes from the here and now, from sharing activities, enjoying a good dinner or country walk. But at the same time you have only just met this person, and if you came into contact in a proactive context such as Internet dating, you probably have very little hard information, the kinds of things you need to know in order to feel the relationship has a chance. While some of this information may have already come out in your phone and email contact, if there is anything you are not clear about, ask again, this time with eye contact. And be forthcoming yourself: volunteer information you think may be important, without being overwhelming. Be open to questions from the other person: after all, they don't know who you are either.

This is as good a place as any to mention that you should at some point make sure that your date is actually who they say they are. While it is very unlikely that you will be unlucky enough to get involved with a con artist or someone with a weak relationship with reality (nice way of saying crazy), it does happen. Make sure you have a landline number for them, and use it. Many people show up on Google these days, especially if they have any kind of professional job, so you can do a Google search to verify their identity. Find out where they live and work, and verify that these are legitimate.

When Cherry was seeing Mark, a doctor whom she dated for some considerable time, the question about identity hovered in her mind:

*The first time he pulled out a credit card and I saw his name on it, was about three months after we'd met. Even though I was confident that he was genuine, it was a relief to see it. And shortly afterwards, when we went to a party together and encountered a mutual friend, it made a real difference to meet someone who knew us both. You can feel that you're existing in some kind of strange, free-floating bubble with someone until you establish links to their identity. I wouldn't necessarily recommend asking for ID on a first date, but I would suggest getting a toehold in each other's worlds before too long.*

Don't worry overmuch about this: just use your common sense and if something seems odd, or too good to be true, keep your eyes and ears open. Subterfuge can more easily happen online, where people can invent whole identities. This is why we advise that you don't persist in an online relationship for long before meeting the person. We do know of one poor man who was involved with someone claiming to be an attractive younger woman in need of help (both emotional and financial) who lived at the other end of the country. Their relationship persisted through email and the phone for several years before he found out that she and her problems were entirely fictitious.

While it is very rare to meet someone on a date who is not at all who they say they are, it is more common to meet someone who is not living exactly how they say they are. Claudia went out with one man who claimed to be single but never invited her to his home. Eventually she discovered he was living with a partner.

The more authentic you are yourself, the less likely you are to attract or be attracted to a deceptive situation. But we can all be duped, no matter how clear and experienced we are, and we are particularly vulnerable when it comes to matters of the heart. So don't be afraid to ask questions if something strikes you as unclear or odd.

## What You Need to Know

- Is the other person seeing anyone else? You may agree mutually to see other people in a friendly way until your own relationship together gels, but you need to know if he or she is actually involved, emotionally and/or sexually, with someone else.

- Is the other person really free? If they are seriously involved with someone else, it will be much easier for you to walk away now than later. Sometimes people put out feelers for a new relationship before ending the previous one. This can result in a confusing triangle that you might not want to be a part of. If you really like this person and think the two of you have potential, you can suggest they get in touch with you again once they are properly disentangled.

- What is their track record of relationships? Is there evidence that they have had a steady and fulfilled relationship in the past? If not, it may be harder for them to commit successfully now. Listen to bad-luck stories sympathetically, but do not necessarily take them at face value. Remember, you're only hearing their side of the story. At the same time, don't write someone off because they haven't been married or coupled in the long term before. Bear in mind that some of us take longer to feel ready to give more attention to relating than to work, for example. And single parents may have been putting all of their relationship energy into raising their children.

- Have they recently had a break-up or bereavement? If so, you may need to develop the relationship slowly. People often think they are ready for a new relationship long before they really are.

- What kind of relationship do you each want? What are your expectations of how a relationship should develop?

- Once you know more about the other person's situation, sift it all through carefully in your mind. Are there any other particular questions that you need to ask, or gaps you want to fill?

## What to Do, and When?

We live in an age with only the vaguest of rules regarding relationships. We have a lot of freedom these days, but with this comes the responsibility for communicating clearly and being thoughtful about how and when the relationship develops.

Two people getting together may have different expectations about timing, commitment, fidelity and contributions of energy, money and attention. Add into the mix the realities of midlife – children, jobs and other commitments – and the whole stew can become quite complicated.

When Lara and James first met, circumstances allowed them to spend some wonderful time together, and their relationship blossomed. But after a couple of months it became difficult to find time to be together.

*He had a very demanding job, two daughters in their early 20s still sometimes living at home, and an ex-wife who used to come back to stay quite often with her partner. So James was constantly surrounded by people and never felt lonely. I was living alone and also working from home, and wanted company in the evenings. So his need to spend time with me was much lower than my need to spend time with him. He was so bombarded all the time that what he really needed was to spend some time alone. There was a deep rapport between us and a lot of affection, but I felt we didn't see each other enough and he felt pulled in different directions.*

Adrian and Valerie lived 200 miles apart when they met. He had a business and loved the area he lived in; she had two teenage children still living at home, but didn't like the area she was living in. She wanted to move to where Adrian lived, but couldn't move until her younger child was old enough to go to university. There seemed no point in Adrian uprooting in the meantime, only to turn around again a few years later, so they agreed to wait, and found a way to make it work by spending every other weekend together and all of the school holidays (when Valerie's sons were with their father), and by talking on the phone several times a day. In this way they were able to develop a close bond even though they knew it would be several years before they could actually live together. Both acknowledge that the distance made their meetings special and romantic long past the stage where this might have begun to wear off. Their willingness to create a plan they were both happy with, and to stick with it, was crucial to the success of the relationship.

## What Does a Relationship Mean to You?

It's a good idea, before you get deeply involved, to discuss what being in a relationship means to each of you. What do you mean by a steady relationship? How soon do you feel happy about going to bed together? Would you prefer to be committed to each other before becoming lovers? How do you see your individual future in terms of a long-term relationship?

At this stage you're talking in general terms, and not about this specific relationship, but you're giving each other a lot of information that can either put you off or be reassuring.

While some of your understanding of each other can evolve without big discussions, it's not smart to think that everything will just fall into place on its own. It's all too easy to think that the other person naturally thinks in the same way you do.

## Timing

We each have our own comfort level and process about the speed at which we like intimacy to develop. Some of us get anxious if it doesn't happen fast. Some are more anxious if they can't take their time, and need to feel fully grounded at each step.

It can be helpful to think back to previous relationships and see which of these you tend to do. Do you fall into bed very quickly and then have to catch up emotionally later? Or are you the other away round, dragging your feet and wanting total commitment before you let yourself be vulnerable? Most of us fall between these two extremes, but few of us manage the transition from stranger to intimate in a completely balanced way. That's very understandable, because it is, after all, a complicated dance with few rules. Knowing your tendencies will help you stay relatively grounded and in touch with your own sense of what is right for you as an individual and as part of a couple.

Here are some guidelines for some of the crucial benchmark points in the early development of a relationship.

### When to Invite Someone to Your Home

Before you invite someone to your home you should know that they are who they say they are and that you feel comfortable in their presence.

### How Soon to Become Physically Intimate

This is such an individual matter, and is also determined differently in each relationship. So we can't say too much about it, other than the obvious advice not to push or be pushed into intimacy before you feel ready. If you've been out of the dating scene for a long time, you may be concerned that instant sex is now expected. It isn't, and don't be pressured into thinking that it is, if that's not what you want. It's more usual to wait several weeks or even months before the relationship becomes fully sexual. Yes, you can have passionate sex very early on and it may well be very powerful because of the release of pent-up feeling in finding someone to be intimate with again, but this can be a short-lived phenomenon. Building a real, long-lasting relationship takes time and trust, and if in doubt, it's usually better to hold back from full physical intimacy until you feel sure.

Once you have sex the relationship changes, and you can never go back from that. It is much easier to reject someone you have not been lovers with, so if you have doubts about really wanting to be involved romantically with the person, it's best to keep your distance physically, unless you are looking for a sexual connection only at this stage. In general, it's common sense to get to know each other fairly well before you sleep together.

It can be challenging to open up physically and get naked with someone new in midlife. Body changes can affect self-confidence. This is often worst at the early stage of midlife, when the first real changes become noticeable. After a while, most of us adapt psychologically to the reality of growing older, and as long we take good care of ourselves we can develop an accepting love for our gradually ageing body. And it is gradual. In many cases the face ages more quickly than the rest of the body, and older people can have very beautiful bodies. Different to the body of youth, but nonetheless beautiful, and sexually attractive.

If you are feeling shy about going to bed with a new person, try this exercise. Take off your clothes and look at yourself in the mirror. Notice how you feel. What parts of your body do you like, and which embarrass or repel you? Is there anything you can alter? Do you need to make dietary changes, which will also improve your health? Do you want to exercise more and tone up a little? Then soften your gaze. Focus on what is beautiful about your body. Allow yourself to feel self-love, to look with appreciation at your own body with the generous gaze of a lover.

If you really feel stuck on this issue you may want to talk to a friend or have some counselling to get some encouragement to move forwards. One woman we know was anxious about taking a relationship to the sexual stage after some years of living on her own. 'It's a 60-year-old body that he'll be seeing,' she said to a friend. 'But it's your body,' replied her friend, 'and it's you he's interested in.' This woman then found the courage to cross the abyss and start physical intimacy, and the man she was involved with did indeed love her body. He simply didn't see the things she thought were unattractive. He was too busy focusing on her curves and her soft skin and her warm and loving smile.

Remember that pretty much everyone is more critical of their own body than anyone else is going to be. Focus on the positive.

## How Much Time to Give a New Dating Relationship to Consolidate

Again, this is a very individual issue. Some people, and some relationships, cook very quickly, and full commitment, even marriage, can occur within a few months of meeting. Most of us take longer than this to bond sufficiently with another person, and this can be more true in midlife, with all the considerations involved. A rule of thumb follows the natural cycle of the year: you need to see someone through each of the seasons before you begin to really know them. After two years you will have a good sense of how you work together as a couple, and whether this relationship is going to be good for both of you in the long haul. In the short term, most people seem to have a pretty good idea after the first few dates if they want to go to the next stage, which is exclusivity.

## Baggage

We all have baggage. No one gets to be 40, 50 or 60 without accumulating a past. And if they haven't any baggage, then they've most likely not really been living. Sometimes people advertise on dating sites or in paper ads that they want someone with no baggage. Thus suggests they have little capacity to deal with reality, because baggage is what we all bring to relationships in midlife.

It's not the baggage, it's what we do with it that counts: how we relate to it and whether we can use it to have a better, more awake and alive relationship in the present. Becoming aware of your own baggage can help you make authentic connections with others, and gives you a better chance of sustaining and developing a promising new relationship.

### *Talking about Past Relationships*

There are few things more off-putting than going on a date with someone new who spends the whole time talking about their ex-partner. If they speak positively and at length, you wonder why they are not still together. If it's because they are widowed, you feel there are three of you on the date. And if they speak negatively, and at length, you can feel yourself withdrawing.

When anyone talks negatively about someone else, we associate the negativity with the speaker just as much as with the person of whom they speak. This is because whether or not we are conscious of knowing this, we all understand that it's human nature to project our own negativity on to others. So the man who complains that his wife didn't love him is likely to have a tendency to be distant, neglectful and possibly narcissistic. The woman who complains that her husband was mean with money turns out to be controlling and critical. This is not to say that one might not have been in a difficult marriage, and be genuinely better off without the previous partner – but even if your ex was a walking nightmare don't talk about it on your early dates, and if you have to, make sure you don't put all the blame on to them. If you find this impossible then you might need some more time or some counselling before you'll be ready for a healthy new relationship.

Martin was taken aback when he began dating again and discovered that a number of the women he met had emerged from damaging relationships:

*It went quite badly. I was surprised at the number of women signed up who'd actually been in an abusive relationship – physical abuse, mental abuse. Once, it became obvious during an introductory phone call that a woman was very bitter about her past. I recall writing against her name 'Never!'*

Lara corresponded briefly with a man through an Internet site who said in his first email to her that he had been badly hurt in the past. But he himself was hurtful in his communication style, and in the next email denigrated her work with a negative comment about psychotherapy. When she ended the correspondence shortly afterwards, he became verbally abusive towards her.

So be careful with people who are clearly still nursing a sense of injustice and hurt. As for yourself, we don't suggest that you should conceal your past or put on a false attitude when meeting someone new, but things will go better if you enter the new relationship with a good heart, and with a certain degree of detachment from previous relationships.

## *Talking about This Relationship*

Don't go overboard too soon in talking about this new relationship. It can kill a burgeoning relationship to try to fix it in stone before it has begun to reveal itself. This can happen especially if one person is anxious to nail the relationship down before it has had a chance to develop. It's like telling a child what they are like based on your own projection and fantasy, rather than letting them develop into their own person.

If you decide the relationship is not for you, however, then don't drag it out in order to save the other person's feelings. You're not helping them: it's kinder to let go so that they can look for someone who really does like them. If you're in the early stages you don't need to give a reason for ending things. Just be pleasant and say that you don't feel you have enough in common, or that you don't feel enough of a spark.

When Jessica was dating, before she met Evan, she developed a graceful way of letting suitors down. She would say at the end of the date, 'Thank you very much, I'm going to see how I feel and I'll get back to you about whether or not I would like to see you again, if you feel the same way.' Then she would give herself several days for the date to 'settle', and if she felt she didn't want to see the person again, she would send them an email saying that she had listened to the wisdom of her heart and it didn't encourage her to continue. You can't argue with the wisdom of someone else's heart, and it's much less upsetting and much less personal than if she'd said, 'I don't want to see you again because I didn't fancy you and you were boring.'

Stephanie preferred a more instant approach: 'At the end of the date I would say, "Are we going to meet again? How do you feel about meeting again?" and see what they said.' One problem with this method is that some people will be polite and say yes, they'd like to meet up again, so you won't necessarily get an honest response.

If Stephanie wasn't interested in following up, she'd say: 'I don't think this is going to work out,' and thank them pleasantly for the date. By doing this, she didn't give herself time to consider things, but the upside was that she didn't have to contact them again. And sometimes you just know almost instantaneously that it won't work out and there's no point beating about the bush.

Whatever your preferred approach, it's more respectful to say something than simply not to make contact again. Unlike with random-feeling emails from people you've never met, this time you have had a real encounter with a real person, and it can be hurtful to be dropped without a word. If you don't communicate, the other person doesn't know whether to keep you in mind as a possibility or to let you go.

If it's the other way round – if you like someone but sense they are not that enthusiastic about you, help the situation along by asking them. Maybe they really like you but are just shy or inhibited. Maybe they are still processing hurt from a previous relationship and need more time before they dive headlong into a new one. Whatever the cause for their reticence, try to find out if it's because you, in some crucial non-negotiable way, don't suit them. In which case, move on. There are indeed plenty more fish in the sea.

## The Information Pool

The early stages of romance can tell us a great deal about the potential for the relationship if we look carefully at the signs and signals that occur around initial meetings.

We have access to information about a new love not only from what they tell us and from our own common sense, but also from the world around us. Paying attention to apparent accidents and strange occurrences (sometimes called synchronicities) can be illuminating and helpful.

The unconscious mind gets very active when we meet someone who affects us, and to whom we are attracted. Our inner knowing can speak to us through dreams, spontaneous intuitions and images, and through body feelings.

All of these sources, from within and without, give us a pool of information that we can use to navigate the early stages of romance and determine if this coupling has a future and if it should be given a real chance. Paying attention to the information pool doesn't mean thinking that every little occurrence is a cosmic message, but rather noticing the ones that have a strong resonance for you. It can be helpful to write down your dreams and any out-of-the-ordinary happenings in your dating journal.

We've had many experiences of the information pool, and here are some examples from our own lives, and how we dealt with them.

## Omens and Portents

Mishaps on dates show us how people respond under stress, which is very useful information. In addition, the nature of the accident or mysterious event can tell us what we need to know about our connection, or lack of, with this new person.

*Lara: I went on a second date with Don a few days after our first short date over afternoon tea. Against my usual practice I had agreed to go on the second date with him while still on the first date. I didn't really want to see him again but felt I had made the commitment, and we did have several interests in common. He had invited me to dinner, saying he loved to cook, and as he lived within walking distance, I thought I might as well go.*

*Shortly after I arrived he beckoned me to the window and said, 'Hey, look at the river.' It was a pretty scene, a boat going past as the sun set. The sash on the window was broken and he was holding it up over me, and then all of a sudden, he let it go and it crashed down onto my head. 'Oh no,' he said, 'I thought you weren't underneath it any more.'*

*It was a genuine mistake, but not a good start. He used it as an excuse to massage my neck and shoulders rather too sensually for my comfort level. It was too soon for physical contact, for me, and I soon stopped him.*

*Then we sat down to dinner, and as we did one of the candles in the candelabra hanging over the table split in two and wax rained down all over the table. We cleaned it up, but Don was so distraught about any residual wax spoiling the table that he talked about it all through dinner and then ran out to get polish and spray cleaner, and cleaned the table while I was still eating.*

*These two incidents, plus his reactions to them, were a clear sign to me that I was in the wrong place and should leave, which I did, as soon as I could, and I didn't see him again.*

**Cherry:** *Randal and I had been seeing each other for a couple of months, and our relationship was confused, to say the least. He didn't know if he wanted to put things onto a more solid footing with me, and in my heart of hearts I wasn't sure either. He was considering a career move which would take him way out of reach geographically, and commit him to an intensive work project for a year or so. Neither of us was keen on the idea of a long-distance relationship, but we were both still wondering if there was something to save from our connection.*

*He arrived at my house on a Sunday lunchtime, on his way up to London to have his final job interview. Although we had planned a relaxed few hours together, it didn't happen. We started to argue about the situation, and the friction that had been there even in our first phone calls came out in full force. Finally we reached what felt like a resolution, and agreed to go on seeing each other as and when it would be possible.*

*I started to cook lunch and while I was cooking, Randal offered to mend a beautiful golden ceramic bowl of mine which had split in two a few days before. He was a skilled handyman, and I had superglue at the ready. But, try as he might, the two sides would not bond. He gave up the attempt, and left after lunch. Later it dawned on me that the bowl showed us what we couldn't grasp in the moment: we simply weren't meant to bond together. As it turned out, I never heard from him again. Some time later I stuck the bowl together myself, with no trouble, using the same superglue.*

## Dreams

***Lara:*** *The night before I met James for the first time, I dreamed I was living in a big house full of books with a big room I had never visited before. I met a man there and together we went to visit an island and he fed me a wonderful meal. It was a beautiful and mysterious dream.*

*After our second date, two friends of mine living in other countries dreamed about specifics of the date (not knowing even that I was seeing anyone) and were so moved that they emailed me to tell me they were sure I was with a new man who would be a very special person in my life.*

*I thought, well, no matter what happens this relationship is important at a soul level, so I should trust that, even though there was a real question over his readiness and emotional availability. And even though the relationship did not become a lasting partnership, in the 18 months we were involved we shared many significant experiences together, including a magical trip to Italy.*

Choosing to follow a relationship because it has a soul dimension and transformative possibilities is an individual choice. There's an equally strong argument for being highly pragmatic and only moving forward with relationships that are clearly workable right from the start. But love is a mystery, midlife is complex, and pragmatism and romance have both to be taken into account. How much weight we assign to each is an individual matter.

*Cherry: A few months before I met Robert I had a dream. In it I met three men who had made a special journey to come and see me, as if from another time and place. I knew that they were my soul companions, companions of the heart. One of the three hugged me in a friendly embrace. We held each other and I sensed a warm current of love flowing between us. The dream ended but the feeling remained, and I knew that it was highly significant.*

*When I met Robert we were both working on a cruise – he was teaching art classes and I was giving lectures. During the time we were on board he had news that his 93-year-old father had died. They had been very close, and his dad had been due to join him on board shortly, so this was quite a shock. The following day I gave him a hug to show my sympathy, and I felt the same warmth and uniting of hearts that I had done in my dream. Some weeks later, after we became a couple, I realized that Robert and the man who visited me in the dream were very similar. There was a quality of soul that suggested to me that they were one and the same. How you explain it is another matter, whether it was a kind of foretelling, a sign that the universe was beginning to reflect back my heart's desire, or perhaps that we really had known each other in another life. Perhaps one shouldn't try to pin these things down too much. But it added to my confidence that we were right for each other, and that our connection was genuine.*

## Spontaneous Thoughts and Images

Your imagination may throw up images spontaneously that tell you something important about the relationship.

**Lara:** *I once had a long-distance phone connection with someone who was a friend of a friend who had initially phoned me for some advice about an organization I was involved with. We liked each other's voices and what we each had to say, and so we began a phone friendship. After a few months his work brought him to a city not too far from where I was living, and we arranged to meet up for dinner.*

*It was a long drive, and on the way I was troubled by an image of him cutting my head off! I thought this was very strange, but didn't want to pay it too much attention because I was already attached to the fantasy of this new relationship developing into something long-lasting. He had such a great voice, and did very interesting work. We had exchanged photos and I had also seen him being interviewed on television, so I knew it was very likely that I would find him physically attractive.*

*The date seemed to be going well and I felt happy and comfortable, and then, about halfway through dinner he dropped a bolt out of the blue. He announced he was seriously involved with someone he had recently met, and that he had met up with me just to make sure that he preferred this other woman, which he realized after spending an hour with me that he did.*

*As you can imagine, my ego took a severe dent, and he did indeed, metaphorically speaking, cut my head off. If I had taken the time to think about the image when it arose, instead of suppressing it because I didn't like it or immediately understand it, I would have been a little more guarded and less taken by surprise when he made his announcement.*

## Body Awareness

We process a lot of information through the body, and physical sensation and energy levels offer us a lot of information about our emotional state. When we begin to become intimate with another person, even if we haven't had sex with them yet, we exchange energy at a subtle level. This can either enliven or deplete us, which gives us clues about the true dynamic of the relationship, and whether it is likely to prove to be a healthy one. However, this can also be complicated by our past experiences such as previous disappointments and betrayals. When the past gets triggered this can affect our energy level.

If you feel unaccountably tired in someone's presence, or when you get home from a date, this usually reflects an imbalance in the energy exchange between you. Either they are taking too much from you, or you are giving too much. Sometimes this can be righted after some thoughtful reflection, and you may find that holding back somewhat, or not answering every one of a barrage of questions will enable you to stay comfortably afloat. But sometimes two people are just basically not a match for one another in this respect.

Cherry found herself exhausted on early dates with Randal, with his nervy energy and his constant talk about sport and keep-fit activity:

*At first I put it down to the fact that I had had some acupuncture treatment that day, which can leave you tired. Then on the next date I decided it was because I hadn't slept well. It was only when Randal himself commented on the fact that I always seemed to be tired when we went out together that I realized something was out of kilter.*

Sometimes a drop in energy can be a sign of an emotion that is not being acknowledged. Instead of being available for you in the usual way, your energy drops because you are using it to keep down a feeling or a knowing. This could be something that would support the relationship, like a positive feeling that you are afraid of because it makes you feel vulnerable. Or you might be having a negative feeling but suppressing it.

- Check your energy and emotional state between dates. Excitement and happiness in the early stages are not necessarily reliable indicators of a good long-term prospect: you may be over-excited because of sexual attraction, because you are being paid a kind of attention you haven't had for a long time, and/or you may be falling in love with love itself, rather than with this actual person. If you are weepy, angry, over-anxious or feel drained at other times, examine whether these states are to do with this relationship or with old material that is being stimulated by being in a new relationship.

- Check how you feel when you think about your next date together. Do you feel joyful, anxious, frightened, indifferent or peaceful? This will tell you something significant about how you are feeling about getting into a new relationship and about this relationship in particular.

- Check how you feel at the moment you next set eyes on your potential partner. A little shyness is natural in the early stages, but if you feel yourself pull back, examine why.

- If you are in a sexual relationship, ask yourself how you feel once the afterglow has worn off. Do you feel complete and quietly content to await the next meeting? Or do you feel needy, even desperate to be back in contact again? There can be several reasons for the latter feeling, but one reason can be that the give and take in sexual and emotional energy isn't evenly balanced between the two of you.

- Pay attention to how you feel in general. Do you feel more content and fulfilled in your own life as a result of the relationship, or less? Other people may say you look happy, which is lovely, but bear in mind that this can occur simply because you have entered the realm of intimacy: it doesn't necessarily mean this person is the one you should stay with for keeps.

Paying attention to the information pool can help you navigate early dates and make it easier to decide whether to persist in seeing someone, or whether to let the relationship go. When we are young, simply fancying someone is often the main pull that gets us involved with a partner, and we often run largely on a biologically-induced instinct. In midlife, our priorities have shifted. By now we have more complex criteria. The information pool can help us become aware of the subtleties involved.

## Staying Grounded

It's a big deal to mix your life up with someone else, and a lot of anxiety can come up in the early stages. How can you make the most of this exciting time and still stay grounded?

Here are several strategies that will help you handle the early days of romance as calmly and healthily as possible.

- Eating nutritiously, not skipping meals and drinking

plenty of water will help your nervous system cope with the excitement of a new relationship.

- Exercising in fresh air, swimming and yoga all work to stabilize and calm the body and mind.

- Meditation not only calms but also opens you to your inner wisdom.

- Psychotherapy or counselling can help ease anxieties and raise your level of awareness about this specific relationship and about your issues in intimate relationships in general. You don't have to be at your wits' end to go to counselling, and it's not a sign of inadequacy to do so.

- Talking with trusted friends and with your dating buddy can help you gain perspective. Sharing some of your feelings, of both joy and of insecurity, is calming, as long as you share only with people who are reasonably well-balanced themselves in matters of the heart. Stay away from the doom-mongers! And also from the complete romantic dreamers.

- Best of all, strengthen your sense of grounding by developing your relationship with yourself, by writing in your journal and taking note of any dreams or intuitions that arise. It helps us to have a good, intimate relationship with a partner when we have a good, clear, open relationship with ourselves. A new relationship brings with it a great opportunity for deepening your self-knowledge, self-love and self-acceptance.

So, to sum up, in the early stages of a potential relationship:

- Allow the romance to flower by going on special dates.

- Ask questions sensitively but without fear. Be open and revealing about yourself, but not overbearingly so.

- Be aware of the lack of social rules governing the early stages of a relationship, and talk about how you both want to proceed.

- Don't go to sleep on your inner knowing or on indications from the world around you. Be awake to all the information available.

- Don't be put off by baggage, but do deal with it constructively and proactively. Again, talk about it and see whether the person is really available or is overwhelmed by pre-existing commitments.

- Stay grounded by enlisting help, and by looking after your physical and mental health.

CHAPTER NINE

# *Moving Forward*

*Peter:* '*It's complicated, love after 40. You can begin to give up, because you've already had many relationships that haven't worked.*'

How do you determine whether to stay involved or to step away and renew your search? Is this new person really right for you, and you for them? Love's famous rose-tinted spectacles are useful for getting us over our edges to intimacy, but we have to put them aside every now and then to stay connected to reality. We each tend to overbalance into hope or fear, optimism or pessimism, and sometimes bounce from one to the other, especially in the early stages of romance.

In this chapter we're going to look at the alchemical nature of relationship, and how to factor this in with your expectations and desires. We explore how expectations based on past experience, either joyful or difficult, can influence your current attitude to love. We discuss how to cope with the inevitable rejections and failures of dating, without losing your optimism and confidence. Then we look in more detail at some special-case scenarios that often crop up in midlife and that can make for hard decisions about whether to stay involved or jump ship.

These special cases are long-distance relationships, people who have been single up to now and have to learn to share and relate intimately, people who are separated but not divorced, relationships with big age differences, and situations in which family demands seem overwhelming.

## The Mysteries of Love

Loving relationships are a dance between keeping some sense of control while letting the magical powers of love and attraction exert their natural and alchemical influence.

Thus, honouring the truth of your feelings can always help you ground, but it won't necessarily give you easy answers. Relationships often take us into paradoxical territory, because we fall in love partly from the unconscious. That's why we feel love 'happens to us'. Things that happen consciously we feel in control of – we make them happen. But love has a mysterious quality that involves opening us up to aspects of ourselves or of life itself that were not necessarily what we had in mind when we set out to find a new partner.

Relationships that look good on paper don't always work out: you make your laundry list of qualities, tick all the boxes, but the reality feels flat. The person you actually fall for usually has some box that is not ticked at all, and/or a quality or life situation that drives you nuts on occasion but expands your life and your being in some crucial way.

Sometimes you won't feel in control, and this is a normal part of love and relationships. Expecting a relationship to function predictably, like a machine, is a fast track to either a lonely old age or an embattled home front. Expecting love to deliver the perfect person is like thinking every day should feel like Christmas: it's only possible if your idea of perfection includes the unexpected and occasionally annoying.

So if you meet someone you really like and feel deeply drawn to, whom you laugh with and love to spend time with, but they have an aspect to their lives that makes you balk (children, money problems, dependent parents, etc.), you may want to give things time, to see if there's a way this apparent problem actually adds some depth to your own life.

When Jessica first met Evan, she thought, 'Oh no, this is never going to work.' She was put off by Evan's boisterous young son and shaky finances following his divorce. 'I don't have kids, I don't want kids, and I don't need a man who is broke.' But there was a deep connection between them that felt very soulful, and she quickly found herself falling in love with him despite her reservations. Now, two years later, she still finds it hard at times that she has to accommodate a child, an ex and the stresses and strains of the situation. But she says:

*I realized recently that I am being stretched to love more unconditionally than ever before, that I have to give to the situation, as a step-parent and partner to a parent. It requires taking the long-term view and being patient and investing in the situation while not necessarily getting everything I want right now. The situation represents a certain aspect of life that I've somehow managed to avoid until now. I've been on my inner journey first and foremost, and quite independent really.*

It's often the case that we fall in love with someone who will stretch us in the way we next need to be stretched for our own wholeness, our own development. The partner who is sometimes distant is actually giving us space to do our own thing; the one who has lots of needs helps us find the generous and giving side of our nature.

## Romantic Expectations

Our expectations clearly influence our decision to stay in or leave a burgeoning relationship. Many relationships founder because expectations are unreasonable. Men are not white knights on horses who jump to every command; women are not princesses in towers waiting to be rescued and then offering their lifelong devotion.

Then there are physical expectations: we're in midlife now, and expecting someone to have the physique they had in their 20s is simply unrealistic and unfair.

It's worth thinking about what your expectations are and where you got them from. Are they relevant to the period and ways in which you live? Often our views about marriage are based initially on our parents' relationship (for good or ill). We also draw from romantic movies and literature when forming our ideas about love.

Once we know what our expectations are and where they came from, we have more freedom to decide what is really important to us. Our parents may have expected a partner with a traditional attitude to roles within the family, whereas we may actually be happier to share tasks fairly equally. Love in the movies is all very inspiring, but real life is grittier and demands qualities that don't always make for good drama.

Knowing yourself in this way will help you communicate with your partner and understand how well your expectations both for romance and daily life actually coincide, and where you need to negotiate. If your needs genuinely fail to be met in this relationship, you may need to part ways and look for someone who suits you better.

If you fell heavily in love when you were young, with the utter intoxication of youth, you may have made this experience your inner blueprint, your litmus test of love. You may therefore expect that for a relationship to work, it has to feel like this again.

If you don't have the same intensity of feelings this time around, you may feel this means that the new relationship is not valid. But this needs to be thought through. In fact, successful midlife relationships are often characterized by a different kind of love, one that is more about calm and mutual support than mad passion. As hormone levels change in midlife so our emotions become more tempered, and our sexual urge calms down. A lot of that mad falling in love of youth is hormonally driven.

How do you know you love someone at this stage in life? It's no longer so much about your knees knocking, your heart rate going up, your face flushing when they walk in the room. It's not about a desperate need to feel their flesh against yours and a sense that you will expire without them. We can sometimes recapitulate our early experience by falling for someone much younger or where the attraction is mainly sexual, but relationships based on lust tend to be affairs and not marriages, and usually blow themselves out after a year or two.

*Peter: It's not being head over heels. I think it's healthy. It's nowhere near any of the other passionate and deliriously emotional connections I had in the past with people who turned out to be a disappointment. If you're madly in love you either go crazy or drive each other away.*

*A relationship that's going to be sustainable over a long period of time burns with a different flame. It needs to be a steady attachment. But sometimes people use the fact they are not madly in love to avoid relationships that might actually work.*

If you want a lasting relationship, then a feeling of mutual calm and well being in each other's company is a more reliable indicator of long-term success than mad passion. This is not to say you won't be excited and passionate about your new love, and indeed it's possible to fall more deeply in love in midlife than when we were younger, because we may have more access to our emotions and appreciate the sense of connection more fully.

**Bella:** *I think emotion and passion can become heightened when you're older, because they can come as such a surprise. You expect to be emotional and passionate when you're younger, and when it hits you when you're older … the surprise is like a wonderful gift.*

## What Friends and Relations Say

Once you have had a few dates with someone, you are likely to introduce them to some of the people in your circle, and vice versa. While friends and relations can be a crucial support during the dating process, they can also be influenced by their own criteria, and not by yours. Maybe their expectations are too high. Are they projecting their need for a perfect partner on to you? If you have been hurt in the past, they may be over-protective. Friends and family members who have a vested interest in you staying available to them may be unfairly negative about your partner.

By the same token, support from friends and relatives can

help you feel good about a new partner. It's very reassuring to know that your friends and family like this person and consider them a good addition to your life.

And if there is a real problem, these people who know you well and love you will be there for you if you have to go through a break-up, and will help you figure out if it's more work that is required, or just walking away.

## Dealing with Disappointment

What if either you or the other person decides not to move forward? Very few people meet their life partner on the first date of their new midlife quest. For most of us it is a process of exploration, and sometimes of dealing with disappointment or even heartbreak.

Allowing yourself to be transformed in the crucible of a relationship means willingly entering the fire of the process. In this way disappointments are fuel for your awakening, to cook you into someone who can actually handle a long-term relationship.

If you learn through the dating process to take disappointment in your stride, you'll do better in the relationship that you eventually commit to.

Let's look at the word: dis-appointment. It's a date (appointment) that doesn't turn out like we had hoped.

There's really no way to protect yourself from disappointment other than to be realistic about how likely it is that you will experience it.

Put a sign with 'Don't take it personally' on your fridge, and use it as a mantra to get you through bad dates and people who seem like a possibility but then disappear on you.

Pay attention to what people tell you right at the beginning. We usually say what really needs to be said very early on. One man told Lara, in the midst of romancing her with great intensity, 'I've always been with women who are totally chaotic. You're much more organized than I am used to.' This sounded like a compliment, but actually he was saying that her style of living was unfamiliar to him and that he was happier with a different kind of person. He completely disappeared a week later.

## How Past Disappointments Can Affect the Present

Many of us come to our midlife relationship quest with a case of what one could call post-traumatic relationship syndrome. Betrayal, abandonment and cruelty are at the harshest end of the relationship failure spectrum, but even frustration and coolness can leave us feeling defeated and low in confidence. A good relationship now can help heal us of past hurts, but at the same time those past hurts can have an impact on our ability to form a new relationship. Unprocessed and unacknowledged pain from the past can infect and hamper current situations. So it's a good idea to deal with this head on, and if necessary seek some help.

**Kate:** *'If you've had a long marriage and it hasn't worked out, you're protective of yourself and can be frightened to let someone in.'*

When Peter met Anna he felt reluctant to get involved because of their big age difference. 'Beyond 40, and especially after major disappointments, you can become so picky, so critical, that anything you can identify as a red flag, you let it put you off.'

We often invest a great deal in relationships, and if they haven't worked out in the past, then the new relationship (and by inference the new partner) has to be pretty perfect to justify previous failures. Also, we can seek perfection in the hope that this will protect us from any further hurt.

Peter acknowledges, 'I was getting to the point where I was in danger of not being able to get close to anybody.' Fortunately for him, Anna was persistent and her certainty overrode his doubts.

The first step in healing is to recognize that you have been traumatized. Some people shrug off hurts easily; others find it very difficult to move on. If you find yourself still angry at a past partner, still dreaming about them, still wishing it had worked out, still surrounding yourself with their things or photographs, then you need to take some active steps if you want to get into a new relationship.

This kind of attachment to the past can really trip up a new connection: you will compare the new partner to the old one, and imagine they might hurt you in the same way, or over-compensate by thinking they will – or should – never hurt you at all. Either way, it's not about the reality of the current moment. You may be overly hard on the new partner, demanding a standard of perfection that no human could achieve. You may find it hard to see them for who they really are. You may have become suspicious, especially if you were betrayed in the past.

Very few of us get through life without being deceived. Betrayals of various kinds happen. Sometimes they occur because we are inadequate to the task of honesty within a relationship, sometimes because life's circumstances are complex and we

202 • Moving Forward

lack the skills to deal with them well, sometimes because we are thoughtless or inconsiderate, and sometimes because people are actually so messed up inside that they enjoy getting one over on others by cheating on them. Most of the time, though, betrayals are distressing for everyone concerned, and can take a long time to recover from.

If we let a betrayal stop us from having love in our lives, we're betraying the needs of our own hearts. We can't build trust in another unless we decide to let them show us they are trustworthy by trusting them first. If you go into relationships distrustfully, then it makes it very hard to get anything off the ground.

Are you trustworthy yourself? Do you trust yourself to make good decisions? Often when we have been hurt, this can erode our trust in our own ability to be attracted to someone who will be a good partner.

## Rebuilding Trust in Love

There are several steps to rebuilding trust. Often we go through these steps without really noticing, and naturally find ourselves open and ready to be vulnerable again. But an accumulation of hurts, or a particularly devastating betrayal, can leave us reeling and unable to open up again.

- Recapitulate what happened. You can do this on your own by writing in your journal, but often it's a more effective process to talk about it with someone who is a good listener. This can elicit a greater degree of clarity.

- Acknowledge how you were hurt or disappointed. Look at it entirely from your own point of view.

- Then think about it from the other person's point of view. Take responsibility for the ways in which you weren't there for them either.

- Did indeed anything 'go wrong'? Or were your expectations simply not met? See the relationship from an objective perspective, as if you are looking down from above. Did these two people have a chance? What could they have done differently, if anything? Did it all work out for the best in the long run?

It's when we have a realistic and philosophical perspective that we know we are ready to get deeply involved again. But don't try to leap to objectivity immediately: feel and acknowledge the emotions involved first.

## Journal Exercise to Process Disappointment and Betrayal

Write down all the people who you feel have disappointed or hurt you in your life. Now write down all the people whom you are aware you have disappointed or hurt.

The list will often be about the same length.

If you find you have been disappointed or hurt far more often than you have caused such feelings, it's time to think about your expectations of others, and your choices of whom you get involved with.

If you find the list of those you have disappointed is far longer than the list of those who have disappointed you, you should look at whether you have a pattern of selfishness and neglect in your relationships.

When you investigate the times you have disappointed others you will find that, most of the time, it was because they wanted something from you that you simply weren't able to give. Consider where this is also true of those who have disappointed you.

## Coping with Being Dumped

It's no fun being dumped. But it often happens when you are involved in proactive dating, because you are putting yourself out there, making yourself available for dates, and not everyone you meet is going to want to continue the connection. Here are some tips for dealing with this situation constructively and not letting it affect you adversely.

- Protect your self-esteem by talking over what happened with someone who knows you well and loves you.

- In order to learn from the experience, recapitulate the dates or phone calls you had with the person. Was there anything in your behaviour that you could change for the future? First-date nerves can make people either too talkative or tongue-tied.

- Check into your memory of your encounters to see if there was a signal you missed. Did they say something to indicate that you were not what they were looking for? Or that they were simply not ready? Was there a signal from your own inner knowing or in the world around that this was not the right path to take?

- If the withdrawal was mysterious to you, don't dwell on it. The dumping may have had nothing to do with you or anything you did or did not do, and may have been all to do with the other person.

- Consider your own side of things: are any unresolved issues from previous relationships being stimulated by this present experience? If so, any new (hopefully superficial) wound is a valuable opportunity to free yourself of old hurts.

- Should you give yourself time to heal? Or get straight back in the saddle? While this is a matter of individual temperament, if you've only seen the person a few times, you will probably be able to move straight back into dating. (This is why it can be a good idea to date several people at once until you decide to be exclusive with one). If it's been longer than a few dates and if you had already become intimate and exclusive, you may need time out. Don't push yourself to date before you are ready, but at the same time don't waste months or years grieving over the past when you need to be getting on with the present.

- See the positive in your experience: what did you learn and gain from this encounter or relationship? Would you approach it differently next time? Write down anything you have discovered. You may be surprised how much wisdom you have distilled from your experience.

- Accept that this is an ongoing learning process and don't expect to know all the answers. Above all, don't criticize yourself mercilessly or consider yourself to be a hopeless failure in love. There are lots of lovely people out there. The moment you feel ready you'll get back out and start meeting them.

## How to End a New Romance

What if it's you who wants to end things? How do you do that without feeling horrible?

Say you've been seeing someone for a while, and you like them but you know something is missing. Maybe you really like them but have this nagging feeling that something is wrong. This will show itself if you feel increasingly reluctant to make plans with them or to become more intimate. Maybe they did something on a date that really put you off and you feel it's not something that can be discussed and worked through. Or perhaps you've been seeing several people at once, and there is someone else you would rather get serious with.

For whatever reason, you've decided that this particular connection isn't one you want to pursue. How do you let the other person down gently? How would you like this to be done to you?

Most of us would rather be told than left dangling. Clarity always helps us to move forward. We're not always totally clear in the territory of new relationships, but at least we can communicate about what we're not clear about. And once you are sure it's not going to move forward, speak!

- It's important to treat others with respect and treat them as you would wish to be treated. So don't give them a long list of what you consider to be their faults.

- Be kind. Be straightforward. Be truthful. Don't say it's because you need time to yourself if really you've met someone you like better.

- Acknowledge what's been good about the connection, and wish them well in their quest for love.

- Don't forget to look after yourself at the same time. It can be upsetting to have to end a relationship, even a relatively new one. It's still a disappointment, even if you were the one who ended things. Keep your spirits up and arrange some new dates.

## Special Cases

Some instances need special handling, and the usual rules or guidelines need to be adjusted to suit the situation. Here are some of the most frequently experienced special-case scenarios in midlife.

### Long-distance Dating

Many relationships that begin through Internet dating or personal ads start off as long-distance connections. This isn't all a bad thing: it gives you time to get to know each other and to adjust to the realities of a new relationship gradually. But there are some inherent difficulties: depending on the extent of the distance, the relationship often takes place in an unreal setting, like always being on holiday, or one of you is working and the other is waiting for them to get off work. It's never the usual day-to-day routine, because one of you is far from home. This can add to the excitement, but can also create discord.

Watch out for people who have had a string of long-distance relationships. They may actually be wary of intimacy and prefer the space that long-distance relationship gives them. Regular contact might not be their thing, so if that's what you are looking for, this may be a frustrating partner for you.

If you do decide to keep moving forward with a long-distance connection, talk together about how you can make this work. The couples we spoke with who were managing a long-distance relationship successfully did it by daily contact through email, texting or phone calls, and by making clear plans in advance of when they would see each other. And when you do get together, build up to longer periods of time. You need to be with someone for more than a couple of days to see what it's like when you get really relaxed around each other.

*Valerie: It's swings and roundabouts – it means we miss each other a lot when we're apart, but when we do see each other it's quite intense. We respond in different ways. Adrian misses me a lot at first and then settles down to being alone again, and I'm the opposite. I get more and more distressed over time. It's important that we have a plan of when we're going to see each other next, otherwise I find the distance just too hard.*

*Adrian: One time, I was supposed to go up at night, and I just felt too tired to drive and phoned to say I'd come up the next day instead. But in fact after I had slept for half an hour I woke up and felt okay and decided to drive up anyway. I phoned Valerie on my mobile while standing outside her house, and pretended I was still in Devon. Then pressed the doorbell, and she said, 'Hang on, there's someone at the door.' She was still talking to me on the phone as she opened the door and her face was such a picture – complete confusion and disbelief. It was so exciting.*

*The Person Who Has Always Been Single Up Until Now*
While someone who has always been single and only had fairly casual relationships may not seem like a good bet, this is not always the case, and it's good to look at the whole picture. Sometimes people have developed relationship skills in other capacities. Adrian had been a monk for 17 years, and since coming back into secular life had had two relationships, but both had been long-distance. On the face of things, Valerie could have been put off by his apparent lack of experience in relationships, but in fact the years he had spent in the monastery had been full of relationship learning in the context of getting along with people and developing skills of empathy and sensitivity to others. The two relationships he had had since had shown him what really mattered to him in a relationship, so he was able to recognize the special quality of his interaction with Valerie right from the first date:

*When we met, one of the strongest impressions on me was that we were walking around the centre of Birmingham after visiting the art gallery, and we ended up in a coffee shop, and we both went quiet for a while, and it was so comfortable. That she was comfortable with silence made a huge impression on me, because of my background, all the time I spent in silence in the monastery.*

We develop relationship skills in other contexts than being married, so think about what kind of work the person has done. People in professions and jobs that put them in touch with the public, especially if this has been in an emotional capacity such as counselling or nursing, will have developed relationship skills along the way. Where being single can really be a problem is if the person has had no opportunity to develop skills of sharing and generosity. Whatever our situation, most of us have to relearn how to live with another person if we go through a substantial length of time living alone in between partnerships. Living alone naturally makes us set in our ways and used to having things our own way.

## The Person Who Is Separated But Not Divorced

This is not necessarily a deal-breaker, but tread with care. Sometimes couples break up just to have a breather from each other and to experience their individuality, especially if they got together very young and never had a chance to develop a genuine individuality.

If they have children still at home, there will be powerful reasons for them to re-establish the relationship if they can work through their problems. Be wary of being drawn into a situation like this. Even if the kids have left the nest or there are no children, habit is a strong force and many people in midlife choose habit and the known over the new and unknown.

Many couples break up for a while and then get back together. It can be hurtful, and a waste of time, to get caught in the crossfire. Couples sometimes use third parties to fan the flames of a temporarily exhausted marriage. It is a cliché (but that doesn't make it any less true) that making someone jealous can re-stimulate their awareness of their feelings.

Even if their divorce really does go through, if you met them soon after they separated you may be their rebound relationship. In the first rush of freedom people often think they are ready for a new relationship, and long for one, but in reality we rarely bounce from one serious relationship straight into another one that will last.

So you may be either the rebound lover, or the one who sends them back to their previous mate. Proceed with caution!

You will also inevitably have to deal with comparisons with the partner they have just split up with. Making a comparison is a natural thing to do, but if overdone it is always odious, even when you seem to come out better. It stops you seeing each other as unique individuals.

If you are the one who is separated and feeling desperate to get into a new relationship, you may want to pause and give yourself time to come back to centre after your break-up. Often the best relationship you can have during this phase is with a good friend or a counsellor or psychotherapist. It's a good idea to work through your own part in why the previous relationship foundered, and thus avoid transferring unresolved issues directly onto your next attempt at a loving partnership.

## Age Differences

By midlife we can feasibly get involved with people in a huge age range, from 30 years younger (as in Peter's case) to 30 years older (as in the case of Becky, another friend of ours).

After Kate's 27-year-long marriage ended she met a man through work who was 12 years younger than her:

*We had a relationship for two to three years, but it was a rebound one. It did me a lot of good because my confidence was low following the divorce. I think it affirmed me in some way. But it wasn't right, because we were at different stages in life. He'd never been married but had a young child by a partner, and my son was just getting married. In fact, that was what caused us to look at it all. I began to think, 'I could be a grandmother in a few years.' My son's wedding was the trigger.*

But age-difference relationships can sometimes become long-term commitments and work perfectly well. They can also have important benefits. The man who hasn't had children by 50 may need a younger woman in order to be able to express his desire to be a father. At the same time, it's useful to bear in mind that while wanting children is a genuine urge, having them is not an entitlement. Some men may do better by facing up to the fact of not having children.

Peter freely admits that after his first marriage ended when he was 40, he had found commitment hard:

*I was so disappointed. I couldn't commit but was starved for affection, which led me into a lot of relationships, over 20 in 10 years. Also, I wanted a family, and the women my age often couldn't any more. I didn't want to mechanically seek out a younger woman, which would have felt predatory. There was conflict about wanting a good relationship and also wanting a family. So there was a tragic element, of not wanting to disappoint but nonetheless doing it. I feel sorry for the women who had to experience me being distant.*

*When I met Anna, I was in a lot of doubt because of the 30-year age difference, but she was persistent, and maybe that's just what I needed. It took the pregnancy for me to let go into the relationship. I thought, 'Either I have to run away because this doesn't seem like it should be, or it's the biggest treasure and gift anyone's ever offered me.' It was her persistence that got me to commit, along with the pregnancy. Without that I am convinced I would have gone into old age alone.*

## Family Overwhelm

If you've met someone who still has children living at home, this can make it a challenge to find time to spend together. It also means you're not getting involved with just one person, but with a family and an extended network that will include the ex-partner and perhaps their family, too.

Remember that the kids won't be at home for ever. And that their presence in your life may greatly enhance it. If you yourself have not had children, then finding yourself in a family in midlife may be a welcome development.

It may be difficult initially for the person with the family responsibilities (and this of course may be both of you) to prioritize the relationship. Parents naturally put their children first, and this can be problematic for a new partner. Sometimes after divorce parents compensate by giving their children excessive amounts of attention, by making them central in ways that actually can be bad for children. The parent may be afraid of losing the approval and love of their children. If they only see their children some of the time, that time will be so precious they may not want to include another person.

All of this territory takes conscious attention. In the early stages, try to give plenty of time and space for the families of both partners to adjust to the idea of the relationship. If you are childless and getting involved with a family, don't let your own insecurity make you push for more intimacy than the family is ready for. It's common sense not to bring new partners into a family until you are both fairly sure that the relationship has some kind of future. At the same time, openness is generally good for families, and keeping a lover a secret will only backfire and make children feel they are being excluded. The situation calls for clear boundaries combined with open communication and sensitivity to everyone's needs. If problems persist, seek professional help from a family therapist to assist the transition.

In midlife, existing situations can mean there is a lot to manage when it comes to building a new relationship. Emotional blocks from previous disappointment and heartbreak, family demands and habit patterns can make moving into commitment a difficult process. If there are problems that can't be resolved, walk away gracefully – and keep going with your search. But if there is genuine love and a real bond, then with conscious attention you will find ways to allow in the new love, untainted by past disappointments and assisted by the wisdom born from experience.

In the next chapter we're going to look at some of the issues that arise once you've made your commitment, and at the seven key perspectives that will help and sustain you in your search for lasting love.

## CHAPTER TEN
# *Riding the Waves of Love*

When Jessica met Evan through Match.com after going on more than 60 dates over a four-year period, she was very happy she had at last found someone who seemed so right for her. At the time, she said, 'I am so nervous. I know it could all blow up in my face any moment. I know all the things that can go wrong.'

Both she and Evan spent six months feeling a mixture of joy and terror, both of them worried that what they thought they had found together might turn out to be simply infatuation, lust, or a great big mistake.

They both had a history of being involved with insecure and emotionally demanding people, and were consciously looking for someone who was as kind and giving as they were themselves. But when they found what they were looking for – a loving and balanced person – their past experiences were still present in their emotional reactions. The disappointments and hurts of the past made both of them defensive at times, and understandably guarded against repeating old and painful experiences. Over time, as they came to trust each other, this guardedness wore off.

Jessica and Evan understood the cause of their anxiety, and were determined that it shouldn't get in the way of their growing love for each other. But they also understood that they needed to integrate the anxiety, not push it away or suppress it. So they factored it into the pace at which the relationship developed. They moved much more slowly into sex and commitment than either of them had before, and this slowness honoured the reality of their feelings in a way that gave the relationship a solid foundation of trust.

This foundation of trust is crucial to the longevity of any relationship, but especially so when you have been previously hurt by betrayal, divorce or abandonment. If you push the fearful inner voice away, then it can erupt later in a need to find proof that your partner loves you. Because this need arises from the subconscious, it may come out in a difficult way.

Volatile emotions often arise in the first year or two of a relationship, when past as well as present emotional issues surface. Examples of such behaviour include suddenly erupting with rage, taking everything your partner says very personally, being negative about any idea they have, or going off sex. If any of these behaviours starts to manifest in a relationship, it's time to pause and ask what is really going on. Ask yourself if it is really to do with your partner. Did they do something that disturbed you that you failed to talk about at the time? Or is this really about something else in your life, past or present, that you are not dealing with directly?

When the heart opens to another, we access our earliest feelings, and thus we also experience the vulnerability of the newborn child. We are opening ourselves up, body and soul, and exposing our frailties and needs to another. Small wonder, then, that we may feel as much anxiety as we do ecstasy, and that we are often emotionally labile until we begin to trust and settle into the new relationship.

When this happens in midlife we have the added complications of the demands of this stage in life. It's one thing to fall in love with an individual and to cope with all the issues that raises, and it is quite another to fall in love with someone who has an ex-spouse, children and a demanding job.

Jessica didn't have any children, had never lived with children, and had never really wanted to. As a psychotherapist she spent all her working time in a supportive and emotionally demanding role, and she liked life to be peaceful and quiet when she got home in the evening. Evan had a boisterous young son, Justin, and a much younger and dependent ex-wife who led an erratic lifestyle and found it difficult to plan when she would take care of the child.

Jessica found herself at times reduced to tears by the complications that now erupted regularly in her previously peaceful spare time. This made her reluctant to move in with Evan, and they kept their relationship at a dating level for longer than they would have done otherwise. Interviewed at the time, she said:

*I either feel left out because Justin is not my child and I will never have the bond with him that Evan has, or I feel frustrated and stymied because I can't discipline him in the way I would if I were his mother.*

She could sympathize with Justin's feelings. As a six-year-old, he was dealing with a lot.

*Very understandably, sometimes he's confused by the situation and acts up. When that happens I feel both powerless to help and annoyed by the intrusion into my weekend. Then I feel mean for being annoyed, when after all he's just a kid being passed between very different households with different rules and emotional atmospheres.*

Evan, on the other hand, felt pulled between three different people, all of whom he loved in different ways, and felt responsible for. But by this time he was deeply committed to Jessica, and wanted to do whatever he could to make the situation work. He listened to her with calm openness, held her when she cried with frustration, and took on board her suggestions about Justin's needs for better limits and more clarity.

Over time, with much talking and open sharing of their feelings – even when these weren't particularly pretty – Jessica and Evan felt confident enough to move in together. Jessica found that she could find ways to influence Justin. She began to teach him how to negotiate his needs, and he became more skilful at asking for what he wanted rather than screaming and shouting because he was afraid that he wouldn't be paid attention to.

Jessica discovered that she enjoyed being with a young child, despite her previous lack of experience. Her ability to create a peaceful home was appreciated by both Evan and Justin, neither of whom had lived in a home where that was such a clear intention before.

Evan found that by focusing more on his own feelings rather than on rushing around trying to placate everyone else, he usually knew the right thing to do or say. He discovered that he could deal with matters directly when they arose.

Together, Jessica and Evan found the confidence with each other to talk about issues they had previously found to be explosive with previous partners. 'We naturally communicate well,' says Jessica, 'and we trust each other. So gradually we've figured out how to make this work.'

The complications of the early stages of midlife relationships need to be understood and approached creatively and directly. It's all too easy for promising relationships to founder under the sea of commitments and responsibilities that many people at midlife have to manage. Self-awareness and emotional maturity are key to navigating the early stages of midlife love.

The good news is that by midlife most of us will be developing some of the psychological traits more often associated with the opposite gender, and thus becoming better balanced as individuals. In many cases, women become more even-tempered and practical; men become more sensitive to feelings and have more desire to relate deeply. We usually by now have more understanding of both our own natures and the opposite gender, and so can understand each other and work through difficulties without a lot of drama and upset.

But even with this knowledge, we may run into issues that need extra help. When Jessica felt particularly troubled by her inability to tolerate the complications of Evan's life, she went into therapy to work on this specific matter. This gave her added insight into her own nature, and she felt she had an objective place to discuss the relationship and gain perspective.

Another of our couples, Hannah and Hugh, went to several couples' workshops in the first two years of their relationship to iron out difficulties and to give themselves a supportive space to be really open with each other. This gave them deep confidence that they knew each other well enough to feel fully confident about getting married.

## Time and Timing

We've talked about the question of timing in various contexts, such as when to hold back or move forward, when to urge for more intimacy, when to sit back and give a budding relationship space to develop gradually, or when to end a disappointing one without more waste of time. It's a delicate balance, deciding at what point to be patient and when to be decisive. The pattern this takes depends on individual nature and circumstance. Some people need to go slower, others naturally move faster. Relationships can run into trouble if the two of you are out of step with your pace of developing intimacy, or fail to communicate your needs.

Despite being in love, and confident they had found the right partner, Jessica and Evan, and Hannah and Hugh, took their time making a commitment and merging their lives. Both couples dated for over a year before moving in together. Jessica and Evan married nine months later, two years after they had first met. Hannah and Hugh married 18 months after he moved in with her.

In both cases this sounds simply like they took a sensible amount of time at each stage, but because the individuals involved were already mature and wanted to get on with their lives, it felt to them as if they were being cautious and patient.

Adrian and Valerie still live apart because of the needs of her teenage children and his business. They know it will be another couple of years before they can move in together, but recognize that this is probably right for them. Nonetheless, they are deeply committed, and plan their future with full confidence.

Adrian says, 'I've lived on my own a lot, and I've needed to grow into living with someone slowly. So now, talking about getting married, it's an ongoing conversation, about the implications and considerations.'

They made the decision to marry a year after their first meeting, but haven't yet set a date. Here again, they recognize the wisdom of waiting until they are ready, and are approaching marriage with care and thoughtfulness, giving space for both emotions and practical matters to be fully discussed.

Valerie: 'I still feel a bit nervous about getting married again and I have to keep reminding myself that Adrian and my ex are different people, and there is nothing the same about this at all.'

## *Step Back and Reflect*

Managing timing is also about managing energy, which becomes a significant factor as we get older. We may be bright and energetic in our midlife years, but we won't always have the pace and stamina that we did in our 20s and 30s. New relationships can be high burners of energy, so we need to factor in time for ourselves, to rest and reflect.

We can find ourselves riding strong and challenging emotions in a new relationship which can, as several of our interviewees remarked, send one plunging back into 'teenager mode' with feelings as powerful and compelling as they ever were. The advantage of being older, however, is that although we might have to ride out the storm, it's also possible to use the wisdom gained to step back from it a little, to watch the waves rising and falling, and to wait for calmer moments, knowing that any tumult won't last for ever. Even though we may experience impatience and upsets, we can trust that the often hard-won wisdom of midlife will see us through.

## Love in the 40s

In your 40s there is still the knowledge that half your life might lie ahead of you, and any feeling of urgency about getting involved is likely to focus on getting back on track, on re-establishing a new marriage or family life to replace the one you have lost, or on opening up new horizons, such as starting a new career which you still have time to develop before retirement. For most people this is a healthy, active and energetic phase, and concerns about timing are more to do with juggling different priorities, of children, work and a lover, for instance. The feeling of not having enough time is likely to relate to all the different elements in life at present, rather than concerns about the future running out.

## Love in the 50s

The 50s are very different; women go through the menopause, which can cause a major shift in sense of identity as well as strong physical symptoms. Men, too, have a kind of menopause, though as yet its effects aren't fully researched or understood (more about this later in the chapter). Menopausal women sometimes feel that old age and death are waiting just around the corner, even though they may still look stylish and stunning, and be leading perfectly normal working lives. This feeling usually passes off eventually, but it can be a hard passage and can give a woman the sense of desperately needing to find a new partner, losing no time, as she sees it, before her charms wither.

The 50s for both men and women can feel like the time for one last fling, one last chance to ride a motorbike or go to a rock festival. This can lead to a tendency to grab quickly at what's on offer, or to go for a casual, fun and sexual affair rather than putting a firm focus on the more serious search for a life partner.

It's important that prospective daters try to understand each other and to find out what the other person is looking for, since their aims may be very different at this stage.

## Love in the 60s

The 60s, both in terms of health and general well being, are generally a more stable and enjoyable period, according to medical and psychological studies. We are likely to have got over the hump of the fear of ageing by that time, and to be ready to make the most of the life that lies ahead of us, in more cheerful mode. Good and stable partnerships can often be consolidated at this time, and commitments made are less likely to be broken than in earlier years.

By the 60s, in most cases children will have left home. And usually by this stage we're less caught up in the world of work. So there is more time for a relationship, and for leisure activities that are most pleasurable when shared with a companion.

Couples at this stage often find it easier to merge their lives than in the more complex and demanding 40s and 50s.

The awareness that time is limited can influence relationships as we get into our late 50s and 60s. We know that we are not going to be around for ever, and the temptation is to want a new relationship right now, while there is still time to enjoy life with another person. And yet all living moments can be treasured, and two years of bliss might, to take an extreme example, be more valuable than 20 years of a dull and lukewarm relationship. So it doesn't always pay to be counting up the number of possible years left that we might have for a new partnership.

### Love after 70

We have talked to people in their 70s and 80s who are eager to explore what life has to offer and to find a companion of the heart to share it with, and many of them succeed. Finding love is possible at any age.

## Practical Matters

As you move into the phase of enjoying a settled relationship, practical issues are bound to arise as you consider moving in together, sharing finances or getting married. All this may need long and careful deliberation, and is beyond the scope of this book, but here are a few points to help you decide which direction to go in.

- Allow yourself time as a couple if possible before living together, so that you can enjoy and develop the relationship first before taking on joint responsibilities.

- Remember that two can live more cheaply than one, and sharing the bills can be a relief after coping with all household expenses on your own.

- Be flexible about possible living arrangements. You might want to keep 'two roofs' or live part-time with one another. And do you want to share a bedroom? For some, hot flushes at menopause or heavy snoring from a partner make it more comfortable to have separate sleeping spaces.

- If you do start to cohabit, it's worth consulting a solicitor to find out how this affects each of you in terms of property and finances. Don't rely on hearsay, which is often inaccurate. This isn't always a complex matter, and sometimes a simple letter of agreement is all that's needed to clarify the situation.

- Take the opportunity to explain to any friends, children or relatives what's going on, as they may be concerned for your security in this respect.

- Consider drawing up or redrafting your wills, which is necessary anyway if you are getting married.

- If you are thinking of getting married, check to see if your pension position will be affected, and any other financial or legal arrangements.

- Creating a new life together can bring opportunities to do something different, so consider whether as a couple you might like to move to a new area, run a business or take time out to travel, for instance.

## Love, Sex and Contentment

Settling into a new relationship can be a delightful process in midlife, bringing warmth, companionship, security and, of course, love and sex. People who love in later life are often more considerate to their partner than they were in youth, and value what they have. In the earlier part of life we may see being in a relationship as our due, as something that was bound to happen, whereas later on the renewal of love is appreciated as something truly precious. Among the couples we interviewed and have met who are now in long-term relationships, there was a great sense of contentment and gratitude that they had been able to meet and fall in love.

Sex at this time of life can be immensely rewarding. The physical and emotional sides of our nature have often become more integrated by this time, which can bring exquisite sensations and subtle pleasures not experienced in previous, younger partnerships. 'Take it slow, and enjoy it!' is the advice often given. From the 50s onwards we may need more time to reach the stage of penetration and to climax, but this can be a delight in its own right. It may become less important to complete the act of sex in the usual way; non-penetrative sex and sensual caresses can also be deeply satisfying. There is less pressure to perform, and more scope to enjoy. Allow yourself to be playful, to share laughter and jokes during sex as well as the more intense moments. Sex can be a very rounded experience at this stage of life.

Women often worry that the menopause will reduce their

desire and perhaps render them uninterested in sex, but the general experience of post-menopausal women seems to show the opposite, that desire can be aroused, sex relished, and orgasms be just as powerful, sometimes more so. Perhaps there is not the same fiery sexual drive, but this brings a greater freedom to choose, and to respond to love, as we wish. There is no longer any worry about getting pregnant, and although the menopause phase is often a complex time for women physically and psychologically, over time hormone levels settle down. Most women find that without the ups and downs of the menstrual cycle they have much greater stability of mood and emotion, which makes relationships more harmonious.

The male menopause, more accurately called the andropause, is a similarly complex phase for men, although less understood and less easy to define in terms of when it actually happens. During this phase men sometimes have a period of crisis in which they experience anxiety about failing potency. When they come out of this period, however, they usually are more developed emotionally and have more to give a relationship in terms of feeling and the ability to be deeply caring and intimate.

Keep the doors open to communicate with your partner about sex. Perhaps in earlier relationships you simply made love without question, and felt it was good enough to get by without discussion. If so, your new relationship may be a chance to change old habits for the better. Talking openly about sexual feelings and desires can bring you closer together on all levels.

## Finding and Keeping Midlife Love: Seven Key Perspectives

### 1. Find the Strength to Love Again

The big trick to midlife dating is not to let negativity or loss of self-confidence from past romantic break-ups have an impact on your belief in a better future. But dating is just the beginning: making the step into commitment can bring up fears and trepidation, and can be a time of resistance and inner struggle.

Becoming committed to a new relationship in midlife can mean we have to dig deep. Dating is one thing, but really letting someone into your life – making a life with them – means finding the strength to believe in love again and to trust that a committed partnership can be joyful.

When we enter a new relationship after divorce or bereavement we are in the process of reconstructing a part of our lives that was previously secure. How and to what extent that security was damaged will influence how we get involved again. We are now older and hopefully wiser, so what we build this time around can be stronger than what we had before.

Being strong enough to date and then to commit will pay off big-time as you discover how much better you are at relationships now, and how much deeper you can go in terms of intimacy and connection.

### 2. Open Your Heart, and Take Care of It Too!

When you embark on the process of proactive dating, you do so with romantic dreams and hope in your heart. Even if you think you are worldly-wise, all of us are fools when it comes to love.

Falling in love demands an innocent heart. But the more conscious we are in this process the better we can take care of ourselves, and learn from every experience we have along the way.

Emotional openness makes us vulnerable, and this feeling is all part of the territory. People sometimes think a cynical or detached veneer will protect them, but this doesn't actually work and can put would-be suitors off. Openness is very appealing: it's much easier to fall in love with someone who has an open heart than a closed one.

Letting ourselves be vulnerable means there will most likely be times when we feel hurt. It's a good idea to have a strategy for handling this, rather than just trying to stuff it under the nearest rug, or becoming consumed by it.

When you encounter disappointment, a bad date, a rejection, someone who turns out to be not what you had hoped they were, or not how they presented themselves, let yourself feel the disappointment fully. Then you'll be able to release it and move on. It's crucial to be conscious of the feelings that come up so you can move past them. In this way you won't lose forward momentum and you will be able to avoid bitterness or long-term withdrawal from the realm of relationships.

Take very good care of yourself in the aftermath of a disappointment. Take hot baths, sit in front of an open fire, talk with friends and loved ones: feed your own warmth and let yourself renew in strength.

Disappointment often arises because we missed signals and saw what we wanted to see. We get disappointed when our perspective is coloured by illusion and projection. Being disappointed is a great opportunity to refine your relationship with reality. Which signals did you miss? Were your rose-tinted spectacles on for just a little too long? In this way we learn about ourselves and about others.

Allowing for conscious vulnerability not only allows us to fall in love, but is also crucial to the development of a relationship. If we keep ourselves shielded and don't share our true thoughts and feelings, we prevent intimacy from developing.

### 3. Think outside the Box

We are evolving creatures, and the way you did dating and relationship in the past may not be what you really want now. So a spirit of inquiry and openness serves us well. The way you dated when you were younger may not be appropriate now. In the US it's long been the norm to date several people at once until deciding to be exclusive with one. In the UK and in Europe people have tended to be exclusive earlier.

We think it's a good idea during a period of proactive dating to go out with several people until you decide which one, if any, you want to be exclusive with. This is because meeting people out of the context of everyday life means there is more likelihood of disappointment than there would be if you met someone through work or friends. A known quantity is a more reliable prospect and would have something to lose by behaving badly.

Multiple dating evens out the game, and means you don't get attached too quickly. It helps with your self-confidence and means you will really appreciate the right person when they do show up.

So unless you are absolutely sure, don't make a commitment to one person simply because you think you should. It's okay, and advisable, to date several people until it becomes clear whom you want to be involved with in the long term.

Then, once you have decided to go for it with someone, continue to think outside the box. We may be attracted to someone because of the new perspective they bring to our life, and vice versa. Relationships are vehicles for change: we fall in love with people who also test us and challenge us, who make us grow. So we can't expect to know all the answers to conundrums we encounter in whom and how we love. Sometimes we need simply to stay open to the truth of the relationship and how it might change both people for the better.

Freedom from notions of how a relationship is supposed to be and how it is supposed to develop, allows us to develop clarity about what actually is happening, and we can assess whether or not it is what we want and need.

## 4. Maintain a Balanced View

Do you tend to think about a potential partner or a burgeoning relationship in terms of what you get from the situation, or what you don't get? Both are necessary in order to have a balanced view and to make a grounded decision to stay or move on. But sometimes we overbalance, especially into looking at what is not there.

If you find yourself in an endless loop of complaint about what is wrong with this person and what you don't get, yet somehow find it impossible to leave, try turning your complaint on its head and focus on what you are getting, rather than on what you are not getting.

Then there's the crucial matter of what you are giving. Are you giving your partner what they need and want? Is your natural style of giving received by your partner? Are you being asked to give to the situation in a way that challenges you? Consider if this stretching is asking too much, or if it ultimately could be a good thing for you.

## 5. Become a Romantic Pragmatist

Underneath all of your romantic yearning it's important to stay practical and realistic. Not taking everything personally is a key to this, as is recognizing that everyone, including you, is flawed. Imperfection is built into human nature. The more we try to be what we think of as perfect, the more likely we are to screw up.

Don't expect love to proceed without the occasional bump in the road. Every now and then there will be misunderstandings, bad days, dull evenings, lacklustre sex and conflicting schedules. Tough! This is life. But if you can breathe through these moments, if you can focus on what's good rather than what's not, if you believe you can navigate challenges with grace and skill, if you open on a daily basis to the love in both of your hearts, then you'll be a romantic pragmatist, and all the happier for it.

The romantic pragmatist is patient, and accepts that Rome wasn't built in a day, and that the process of finding a new long-term love may take a while.

The romantic pragmatist sees relationship like any other important aspect of life: something you can get better at if you apply yourself. Thus a bad first marriage doesn't mean you are a hopeless case and doomed to relationship despair. But it might mean you learn simple conflict resolution techniques, or how to talk openly about your feelings, or how to ask for what you need. These are all common ways in which we fail ourselves and our partners in a relationship, and they are all things we can quite easily do something about.

The romantic pragmatist understands that intimacy can be experienced just as well on a rainy day as a sunny one, and that airing one's concerns and having a really open conversation can bring you closer rather than driving you apart.

## 6. Allow the Relationship Time to Develop

As long as you feel fundamentally positive towards the new person in your life, even if you are not 100 per cent sure, it's sensible to give the relationship time to grow and to show you what it can become. Cutting out of slowly blossoming relationships because they don't seem perfect, or don't look like what you had in the past, can mean you walk away from something that could have grown into a really good partnership. But only you know what your really crucial criteria are, and sometimes we only find that out within the context of the relationship itself.

This is where our baggage can really come into play. Either we've been hurt in the past and are overly suspicious now (once burned, twice shy) and/or we have some idyllic memory of how totally we fell in love 20 years ago. If this relationship doesn't rise to those dizzying heights of passion, we think it's not good enough. But as we get older our emotions often soften and change, so that we don't fall in love or become closely involved with the same rapid intensity as when we were young.

Stand back a little, give the new relationship some space, see what it grows into. The kind of love you may find emerging out of this open space could be far more nourishing and sustainable than the passion you experienced in youth.

## 7. Be Yourself and Trust the Journey

We've given you lots of guidelines and suggestions in this book, but everyone has an individual path in love. And that's what's most important. Be yourself! Trust the path of your life. If you've not found a happy relationship yet, remember, you don't know what is around the corner. Keep looking, keep your heart open, and stay open and loving to your life as a whole. This will keep you attractive, and able to recognize new love when it walks into your life.

We began this book with an invitation to proactive dating, to take fate into your own hands and to embark on the search for love. So we don't recommend that you sit around waiting for love to just happen. But at the same time, none of us can push the river, and sometimes life takes longer than we want to bring us what we need. Meanwhile, we have to keep going and be patient and persistent.

Have faith in your journey, and trust that things will work out for the best, both in terms of timing and in terms of bringing you the love that is right for your time of life. It can be tempting to settle for the first person who comes along who ticks a few boxes and whom you think you could rub along with.

Give yourself time. Wait for someone with whom you have

a true connection. There is nothing wrong with marrying for loving companionship rather than passion, but don't sell yourself short. It may be time to put away those unfulfilled romantic dreams of an impossibly gorgeous lover, but it isn't time to give up on finding the right person to share your life with.

So don't settle, but also, don't be a perfectionist. If you've met someone whose company you greatly enjoy, with whom you naturally have a sense of compatibility but there aren't enough fireworks to be absolutely certain this is the love of your life, again, give it time. With everything else that is going on in this stage in life, love in midlife sometimes develops slowly.

If you've met someone you feel you can make a new life with, you'll know that every happy arrival is a new beginning. When you begin to settle into a new relationship you are entering a different phase, with its own dynamics and challenges. We take you to this point, and wish you all the very best for your future together. And for those whose journey towards love and a relationship is still in progress, we wish you great good fortune with your quest, and we keep faith with you that you will find a wonderful love and deep fulfilment in the course of time. May you be blessed with love, and graced with a true companion.

# RESOURCES

## Some Interesting Reading on Dating and Relationships

Gee, Ariana, and Gregory, Mary, *Be Your Own Love Coach: Ways to Help You Find and Keep Your Soulmate* (London: New Holland Publishers, 2005).

Henderson, Lauren, *Jane Austen's Guide to Romance* (London: Headline, 2005) – an entertaining exploration of how Jane Austen got it right when it comes to dating advice.

Hillis, Marjorie, *Live Alone and Like it* (London: Virago Press, 2005) – a quirky, endearing book first published in the 1930s, with tips for the single woman, even if she is only between relationships.

Jones, Maggie, *Marrying an Older Man* (London: Piatkus, 1993) – case histories and thoughtful insights into the age-difference marriage.

Kasl, Charlotte, *If the Buddha Dated: A Handbook for Finding Love on a Spiritual Path* (NY: Penguin, 1999).

Ramsay, Jay, *Crucible of Love: The Alchemy of Passionate Relationships* (Alresford, Hants: O Books, 2004) – an approach to mature relationships using the symbolism of alchemy to explore their dynamics.

*Saga* magazine: relevant articles from this magazine written for the over-50s are frequently posted at www.saga.co.uk/magazine/relationships.

Springett, Ulli, *Soulmate Relationships* (London: Piatkus, 2003) – a compassionate and wise guide to finding a soulmate partner, with good advice on countering loneliness.

# Dating Websites

There are new dating sites springing up every day, and new services being added to existing ones. Here are some of the more established sites that our interviewees used with success.

## *Major Websites*

**Dating Direct:** big site for UK and Europe, now with video calling as well as online chat: www.datingdirect.com

**Friends Reunited:** easy to access for people who are already signed up to the general FR membership: www.friendsreuniteddating.co.uk

**Guardian Soulmates:** run by the *Guardian* newspaper, bonus includes free inclusion in personal-ad section in the weekend paper: dating.guardian.co.uk

**Match.com:** huge international site: match.com

**Meetic.com:** large, pan-European site: meetic.com

**Parship.com:** this is the site used by *The Independent* newspaper in the UK, but is also big in its own right in France and elsewhere. Features an in-depth compatibility profiling programme to match prospective partners: www.parship.co.uk

## *Examples of Smaller, Specialized Sites*

**Countryside Love:** for rural dwellers: www.countryside-love.co.uk

**Dharmamatch:** site for the spiritually inclined: www.dharmamatch.com

**Ivory Towers:** for graduates, also organizes face-to-face events: www.ivorytowers.net

# Introduction Agencies

Association of British Introduction Agencies: listings of member agencies to contact, with details of how they work, and tips on handling dates: www.abia.org.uk

 **Lara Owen** was born in England in 1955. She graduated from the University of Warwick, and then studied Chinese medicine in the UK and China. After several years in practice, she realized her deepest interest lay in her clients' dreams, inner states and relationship issues, and that she also wanted to make time to write. She made a career change and since then has combined writing with psychotherapy.

Lara studied relationship dynamics as part of her five-year training in process-oriented psychology in Switzerland and the US, and has worked with individuals and couples since the early 1990s. She is the author of *Her Blood Is Gold* (later reissued as *Honoring Menstruation*), a groundbreaking book on the psychological and physical effects of cultural attitudes to menstruation. She has lectured internationally on health and spirituality, and on creative writing and creative process.

Lara has travelled widely, and lived on the West Coast of the US for 15 years. She now divides her time between south-west England and south-west France, and works with clients all over the world by phone and online.

For more about Lara and her work, please visit laraowen.com

**Cherry Gilchrist** is an author and lecturer, whose subjects include titles on mythology, divination, the feminine psyche, the Silk Road, and Russian art and culture. Her children's book, *A Calendar of Festivals*, received a UK Reading Award, and *The Elements of Alchemy* (now *Explore Alchemy*) has been translated into several languages. Much of her work is inspired by a love of discovering ancient wisdom, and renewing it in a contemporary context. Cherry also teaches Life Writing, based on a keen interest in personal narrative and family history.

Although Cherry wanted to write from an early age, she has also followed the lure of buying and selling exotic items, first running a vintage clothes shop and in recent times a Russian arts and crafts business. She is fascinated by traditional cultures, and has travelled widely, visiting destinations such as Central Asia, Siberia and South America.

Other interests include singing early music, cooking and country walking. She was married for nearly 30 years, has two grown-up children, and now lives near Stroud in Gloucestershire with her partner, Robert, who is an artist.

Read more about Cherry and her books at www.cherrygilchrist.co.uk

## Titles of Related Interest

*YOU CAN HEAL YOUR LIFE, the movie*, starring Louise L. Hay &
Friends
(available as a 1-DVD set and an expanded 2-DVD set)
Watch the trailer at www.LouiseHayMovie.com

*The Age of Miracles*, by Marianne Williamson
*Feel Happy Now*, by Michael Neill
*Dr Lucy Actcheson's Guide to Perfect Relationships*
*You Can Heal Your Life*, by Louise L. Hay
*Everything I've Ever Learned About Love*, by Lesley Garner